Hugo's Sim

Bulgarian
Phrase Book

Hugo's Language Books Limited

Compiled by
Lexus Ltd
with
Zhivko T Gulaboff

*Facts and figures given in this book were
correct when printed. If you discover any
changes, please write to us.*

Set in 9/9 Plantin by
Lexus Ltd with Dittoprint Ltd, Glasgow

Printed in England by Page Bros., Norwich

CONTENTS

PREFACE

This is the latest in a long line of Hugo phrase books and is of excellent pedigree, having been compiled by experts to meet the general needs of tourists and business travellers. Arranged under the usual headings of 'Hotels', 'Motoring' and so forth, the ample selection of useful words and phrases is supported by a 2,000 line mini-dictionary. By cross-reference to this, scores of additional phrases may be formed. There is also an extensive menu guide listing over 300 dishes or methods of cooking and presentation.

Highlighted sections illustrate some of the replies you may be given and the signs or instructions you may see or hear. The pronunciation of words and phrases in the main text is imitated in English sound syllables, and particular characteristics of Bulgarian are illustrated in the Introduction. You should have no difficulty managing the language, especially if you use our audio-cassette of selected extracts from the book. Ask your bookseller for the Hugo Bulgarian Travel Pack.

INTRODUCTION

PRONUNCIATION

When reading the imitated pronunciation, stress that part which is underlined. Pronounce each syllable as if it formed part of an English word, and you will be understood sufficiently well. Remember the points below, and your pronunciation will be even closer to the correct Bulgarian:

a	as in 'far'
ay	as in 'may'
e	as in 'men'
g	always as in 'go', not as in 'German'
I	as the 'i' sound in 'die'
H	a guttural 'ch' as in the Scottish word 'loch'
o	as in 'cod'
s	as in 'sit'
u	as in 'urgent', only shorter
zh	as the 's' in 'leisure', only harder

The mini-dictionary provides Bulgarian translations in the form of the imitated pronunciation so that you can read the words without reference to the Bulgarian alphabet.

Over the page is a further guide to Bulgarian pronunciation, alongside the Bulgarian (Cyrillic) alphabet.

GENDERS AND ARTICLES

All Bulgarian nouns have one of three genders: masculine, feminine or neuter. You can generally tell the gender of a noun by its ending:

    most masculine nouns end in a consonant:
      e.g. кон *(kon)* horse, стол *(stol)* chair;
    most feminine nouns end in -a:
      e.g. жена *(zhena)* woman, маса *(masa)* table;
    all neuter nouns end in -e:
      e.g. дете *(deteh)* child, име *(imeh)* name.

INTRODUCTION

In Bulgarian, the definite article ('the') is not a separate word, but an ending attached to the noun. This ending changes according to the gender of the noun: the following will help you create the definite form for singular noun endings.

a) masculine* nouns add: -а/-я, *(-a/-ya)*
    e.g. мъж *(mush)* man/a man, мъжа *(muzha)* the man;
    учител *(oochitel)* teacher/a teacher, учителя *(oochitelya)* the teacher.

b) feminine nouns add: -та *(-ta)*
    e.g. жена *(zhena)* woman/a woman, жената *(zhenata)* the woman;
    маса *(masa)* table/a table, масата *(masata)* the table.

c) neuter nouns add: -то *(-to)*
    e.g. дете *(deteh)* child/a child, детето *(deteto)* the child;
    име *(imeh)* name/a name, името *(imeto)* the name.

*There are two forms of the article for masculine nouns: the short form (shown above) and the full form. The full form is used only when the noun is the subject of a sentence, but not in colloquial spoken Bulgarian – when the short form is used in all instances, whether or not the noun is the subject. You could get by without using the full form, but here it is:

d) masculine full form add: -ът/-ят *(-ut/-yat)*
    e.g. мъж *(mush)* man/a man, мъжът *(muzhut)* the man;
    учител *(oochitel)* teacher/a teacher, учителят *(oochitelyat)* the teacher.

There is no indefinite article in Bulgarian; for example, жена *(zhena)* can mean 'woman' or 'a woman'. The word for 'one' can be used for emphasis, but since this changes according to gender (един мъж, *edin mush*, 'a man'; една жена, *edna zhena*, 'a woman'; едно име, *edno imeh*, 'a name') you'll probably avoid using it.

THE BULGARIAN (CYRILLIC) ALPHABET

letter   *pronunciation*

А а	'a' as in 'far'
Б б	'b' as in 'bag'
В в	'v' as in 'van'
Г г	'g' as in 'go'
Д д	'd' as in 'do'
Е е	'e' as in 'men'
Ж ж	'zh' as the 's' in 'leisure'
З з	'z' as in 'zoo'
И и	'i' as in 'bin'
Й й	'y' as in 'boy'
К к	'k' as in 'kin'
Л л	'l' as in 'lap'
М м	'm' as in 'mat'
Н н	'n' as in 'none'
О о	'o' as in 'cod'
П п	'p' as in 'pin'
Р р	similar to the Scottish rolled 'r'
С с	's' as in 'sit'
Т т	't' as in 'tin'
У у	'oo' as on 'boot'
Ф ф	'f' as in 'fun'
Х х	'ch' in the Scottish word 'loch'
Ц ц	'ts' as in 'let's'
Ч ч	'ch' as in 'chin'
Ш ш	'sh' as in 'shore'
Щ щ	'sht' as in the end sound of 'washed'
Ъ ъ	'u' as in 'urgent' only shorter
ь ь	this softens the preceding consonant
Ю ю	'you' as in 'youth' only shorter
Я я	'ya' as in 'yak'

The alternatives (said by a man/woman) in the phrases show the forms to be used by a male or female speaker.

USEFUL EVERYDAY PHRASES

Yes/No
Да/Не
da/neh

Thank you
Благодаря
blagodarya

No thank you
Не, благодаря
neh, blagodarya

Please
Моля
molya

I don't understand
Не разбирам
neh razbiram

Do you speak English/French/German?
Говорите ли английски/френски/немски?
govoriteh li angleeski/frenski/nemski?

I can't speak Bulgarian
Не говоря български
neh govorya bulgarski

I don't know
Не знам
neh znam

Please speak more slowly
Моля, говорете по-бавно
molya, govoreteh po bavno

Please write it down for me
Моля, напишете ми това
molya, napisheteh mi tova

My name is …
Казвам се …
kazvam seh …

How do you do, pleased to meet you
Здравейте, приятно ми е
zdravayteh, pri-yatno mi eh

Good morning
Добро утро
dobro ootro

Good afternoon
Добър ден
dobur den

Good evening
Добър вечер
dobur vecher

Good night *(when going to bed)*
Лека нощ
leka nosht

Good night *(leaving group early)*
Довиждане
dovizhdaneh

Goodbye
Довиждане
dovizhdaneh

How are you?
Как сте?
kak steh?

USEFUL EVERYDAY PHRASES

How are you? *(informal)*
Как си?
kak si?

Excuse me please
Извинете ме, моля
izvineteh meh, molya

Sorry! *(apology)*
Извинете!
izvineteh!

Sorry? *(pardon?)*
Моля?
molya?

I'm really sorry
Много се извинявам
mnogo seh izvinyavam

Can you help me?
Бихте ли ми помогнали?
biHteh li mi pomognali?

Can you tell me ...?
Бихте ли ми казали ...?
biHteh li mi kazali ...?

Can I have ...?
Бихте ли ми дали ...?
biHteh li mi dali ...?

I would like ... *(said by a man/woman)*
Бих искал/искала ...
biH iskal/iskala ...

Is there ... here?
Има ли тук ...?
ima li took ...?

Where can I get ...?
Къде мога да намеря ...?
kudeh moga da namerya ...?

How much is it?
Колко струва?
kolko stroova?

What time is it?
Колко е часът?
kolko eh chasa?

I must go now
Трябва да си ходя
tryabva da si Hodya

I've lost my way
Изгубих се
izgoobiH seh

Cheers! *(toast)*
Наздраве!
nazdraveh!

Do you take credit cards?
Приемате ли кредитни карти?
pri-emateh li kreditni karti?

Where is the toilet?
Къде е тоалетната?
kudeh eh to-aletnata?

Go away!
Оставете ме на мира!
ostaveteh meh na mira!

Excellent!
Чудесно!
choodesno!

11

THINGS YOU'LL SEE

аварен изход	*avari-en isHot*	emergency exit
асансьор	*asansyor*	lift
Балкантурист	*balkantoorist*	Balkantourist
бутни	*bootni*	push
влезте	*vlesteh*	come straight in
вода за пиене	*voda za pi-eneh*	drinking water
вход	*fHot*	way in, entrance
вход забранен	*fHot zabranen*	no admittance
вход за външни	*fHot za vunshni*	private,
лица забранен	*litsa zabranen*	no admittance
вход свободен	*fHot svoboden*	admission free
дава се под наем	*dava seh pod na-em*	to let
дръпни	*drupni*	pull
жени	*zheni*	ladies
заето	*za-eto*	engaged
запазено	*zapazeno*	reserved
затворено	*zatvoreno*	closed
изход	*isHot*	way out
изчакайте	*ischakIteh*	please wait
каса	*kasa*	till, cash desk
мъже	*muzheh*	gents
отворено	*otvoreno*	open
работно време	*rabotno vremeh*	visiting hours,
		opening times
пазете тишина	*pazeteh tishina*	silence, quiet
пази се от боята	*pazi seh ot bo-yata*	wet paint
пожарен изход	*pozharen isHot*	fire exit
продава се	*prodava seh*	for sale
свободно	*svobodno*	vacant
сезонна	*sezonna rasprodazhba*	sale
разпродажба		
тоалетни	*to-aletni*	toilets

THINGS YOU'LL HEAR

blagodarya	Thanks
blagodarya, dobreh	Very well, thank you
– a vi-eh?	– and you?
dovizhdaneh	Goodbye; See you later
izvineteh	Excuse me
kak si?	How are you? *(informal)*
kak steh?	How are you?
molya	You're welcome; Pardon?
neh razbiram	I don't understand
neh znam	I don't know
taka li?	Is that so?
tochno taka	That's right
vnimavi!	Look out!
zapovyaditeh	Here you are
zdravayteh, pri-yatno	How do you do, nice to meet
mi eh	you

DAYS, MONTHS, SEASONS

Sunday	неделя	*nedelya*
Monday	понеделник	*ponedelnik*
Tuesday	вторник	*ftornik*
Wednesday	сряда	*sryada*
Thursday	четвъртък	*chetvurtuk*
Friday	петък	*petuk*
Saturday	събота	*subota*

January	януари	*yanoo-ari*
February	февруари	*fevroo-ari*
March	март	*mart*
April	април	*april*
May	май	*mI*
June	юни	*yooni*
July	юли	*yooli*
August	август	*avgoost*
September	септември	*septemvri*
October	октомври	*oktomvri*
November	ноември	*no-emvri*
December	декември	*dekemvri*

Spring	пролет	*prolet*
Summer	лято	*lyato*
Autumn	есен	*esen*
Winter	зима	*zima*

Christmas	Коледа	*koleda*
Christmas Eve	Бъдни вечер	*budni vecher*
New Year	Нова година	*nova godina*
New Year's Eve	новогодишна нощ	*novogodishna nosht*
Easter	Великден	*velikden*

NUMBERS

0	нула *noola*	16	шестнайсет *shesnIset*
1	едно *edno*	17	седемнайсет *sedemnIset*
2	две *dveh*	18	осемнайсет *osemnIset*
3	три *tri*	19	деветнайсет *devetnIset*
4	четири *chetiri*	20	двайсет *dvIset*
5	пет *pet*	21	двайсет и едно *dvIset i edno*
6	шест *shes*	22	двайсет и две *dvIset i dveh*
7	седем *sedem*	30	трийсет *treeset*
8	осем *osem*	31	трийсет и едно *treeset i edno*
9	девет *devet*	32	трийсет и две *treeset i dveh*
10	десет *deset*	40	четирисет *chetirset*
11	единайсет *edinIset*	50	петдесет *pedeset*
12	дванайсет *dvanIset*	60	шейсет *shayset*
13	тринайсет *trinIset*	70	седемдесет *sedemdeset*
14	четиринайсет *chetirinIset*	80	осемдесет *osemdeset*
15	петнайсет *petnIset*	90	деветдесет *devedeset*

100	сто *sto*	
110	сто и десет *sto i deset*	
200	двеста *dvesta*	
300	триста *trista*	
400	четиристотин *chetiristotin*	
500	петстотин *petstotin*	
600	шестотин *shestotin*	
700	седемстотин *sedemstotin*	
800	осемстотин *osemstotin*	
900	деветстотин *devetstotin*	
1,000	хиляда *Hilyada*	
10,000	десет хиляди *deset Hilyadi*	
20,000	двайсет хиляди *dvIset Hilyadi*	
100,000	сто хиляди *sto Hilyadi*	
1,000,000	милион *mili-on*	

TIME

today	днес	*dnes*
yesterday	вчера	*fchera*
tomorrow	утре	*ootreh*
the day before yesterday	онзи ден	*onzi den*
the day after tomorrow	вдруги ден	*vdroogi den*
this week	тази седмица	*tazi sedmitsa*
last week	миналата седмица	*minalata sedmitsa*
next week	другата седмица	*droogata sedmitsa*
this morning	тази сутрин	*tazi sootrin*
this afternoon	днес следобяд	*dnes sletobyat*
this evening	тази вечер	*tazi vecher*
tonight	довечера	*dovechera*
yesterday afternoon	вчера следобяд	*fchera sletobyat*
last night	снощи	*snoshti*
tomorrow morning	утре сутринта	*ootreh vecher*
in three days	след три дни	*slet tri dni*
three days ago	преди три дни	*predi tri dni*
late	късно	*kusno*
early	рано	*rano*
soon	скоро	*skoro*
later on	по-късно	*po kusno*
at the moment	в момента	*fmomenta*
second	секунда	*sekoonda*
minute	минута	*minoota*
one minute	една минута	*edna minoota*
two minutes	две минути	*dveh minooti*
quarter of an hour	четвърт час	*chetvurt chas*
half an hour	половин час	*polvin chas*
three quarters of an hour	три-четвърти час	*tri chetvurti chas*
hour	час	*chas*
that day	този ден	*tozi den*

16

every day	всеки ден	*fseki den*
all day	цял ден	*tsyal den*
the next day	следващият ден	*sledvashti-ya den*

TELLING THE TIME

To say 'one o'clock', 'two o'clock' etc, place the appropriate number in front of the word **часа** (*chasa*), meaning 'hour'. Some numbers in Bulgarian have different gender forms and the masculine forms for one and two are used for telling the time: 'one o'clock' is **един часа** (*edin chasa*); 'two o'clock' is **два часа** (*dva chasa*). The remaining hours up to twelve o'clock are simply the appropriate number plus the word **часа** (*chasa*).

For time past the hour, e.g. 'ten past five', Bulgarians say **пет и десет** (*pet i deset*), which translated literally means 'five and ten'. Sometimes you may hear the word **четвърт** (*chetvurt*) being used to denote a quarter of an hour – e.g. 'quarter past five' **пет и четвърт** (*pet i chetvurt*), but **пет и петнайсет** (*pet i petnlset*), literally 'five and fifteen', is more common. 'Half past' is **и половина** (*i polovina*), literally 'and half', or **и трийсет** (*i treeset*), 'and thirty'. So 'half past three' can be either **три и половина** or **три и трийсет**.

For time to the hour Bulgarians use **без** (*bes*), meaning 'minus', so 'quarter to' can be translated as **без четвърт** (*bes chetvurt*) or **без петнайсет** (*bes petnlset*). 'Quarter to five' is therefore **пет без четвърт** (*pet bes chetvurt*) or **пет без петнайсет** (*pet bes petnlset*).

Minutes to the hour are expressed as in 'quarter to ...' above, e.g. 'five to three' **три без пет** (*tri bes pet*), literally 'three minus five'. All other expressions of time to the hour are formed following this pattern and there are no exceptions.

In general, the 24-hour clock is more commonly used than in Britain, particularly on radio and TV.

The numbers section on page 15 provides the rest of the numerals necessary for telling the time.

TIME

am	сутрин	*sootrin*
pm	следобед	*sletobet*
one o'clock	един часа	*edin chasa*
ten past one	един и десет	*edin i deset*
quarter past one	един и петнайсет	*edin i petnIset*
half past one	един и половина	*edin i polovina*
twenty to two	два без двайсет	*dva bes dvIset*
quarter to two	два без петнайсет	*dva bes petnIset*
two o'clock	два часа	*dva chasa*
13.00	тринайсет часа	*trinIset chasa*
16.30	шестнайсет и трийсет	*shesnIset i treeset*
at half past five	в пет и половина	*fpet i polovina*
at seven o'clock	в седем часа	*fsedem chasa*
noon	обед	*obet*
midnight	полунощ	*poloonosht*

HOTELS

Until recently all hotels in which a foreigner was likely to stay were owned by the state tour operator Balkantourist. Although this company is currently being privatised, standards and arrangements remain much the same.

Hotels are classified as de luxe, first, second and third category or often (but not necessarily) with stars ranging from * to *****. In city centres there is usually an Interhotel which conforms to the international standards for its category (normally between *** and *****). Most other hotels, however, offer more than adequate accommodation for a fraction of the price that you would pay for an Interhotel room.

Many of the residences and the holiday homes that were once reserved for party apparatchiks are now used as hotels and often provide more extras for the same price as Interhotels.

Most hotels in Bulgaria have at least one restaurant, bar or coffee shop; larger hotels have more facilities such as room service, hairdressing and shopping arcades.

The coastal resorts offer a variety of accommodation – conventional hotel complexes (Costa del Sol-style), purpose-built holiday villages (cottages and bungalows) and old towns with traditional Bulgarian architecture where you can stay in the newly-emerging privately-owned hotels or rent a private room. The latter often come with a landlord or landlady unless you hire a whole villa. Private rooms are usually excellent value for money and are bookable from local tourist offices. Motels and campsites are to be found along the major tourist routes and the coast (see also CAMPING AND CARAVANNING page 26).

Breakfast may be included in the price of the room but this is much less common in Bulgaria than in the West and most likely only to be included with the room price in hotels with three or more stars. The prices for privately-owned rented accommodation generally do not include breakfast.

Bulgarian bathrooms normally only have a shower; baths are usually to be found in hotels with three or more stars. In any case it is a good idea to take a universal bath/sink plug with you since this is the item most likely to be found missing even from luxury hotel bathrooms.

Hotel bills are usually expected to be settled in cash unless you are on a package holiday. Credit cards may be used in some big hotels and shops; this however is not always indicated clearly and it is best to ask before you buy. Cheques (with the exception of travellers' cheques) are rarely accepted. The US dollar is the easiest foreign currency to pay with in Bulgaria; Western tourists are sometimes expected to pay directly in US dollars (although this is never obligatory). This, together with the variable exchange rate, makes it unwise to change large sums into Bulgarian currency at any one time. (See also POST OFFICES AND BANKS, page 82.) Tipping is at the usual rate of around 10%.

USEFUL WORDS AND PHRASES

balcony	балкон	balk_on_
bath (tub)	вана	v_a_na
bathroom	баня	b_a_nya
bed	легло	legl_o_
bedroom	стая	st_I_-a
bill	сметка	sm_e_tka
breakfast	закуска	zak_oo_ska
dinner (evening meal)	вечеря	vech_e_rya
double bed	двойно легло	dv_oy_no legl_o_
double room	двойна стая	dv_oy_na st_I_-a
foyer	фоайе	fwa-y_e_h
full board	пълен пансион	p_u_len pansi-_on_
guesthouse	частен пансион	ch_a_sten pansi-_on_
half board	полупансион	pol_oo_pansi-on
hotel	хотел	Hotel
key	ключ	klyooch
lift	асансьор	asansy_or_
lounge	фоайе	fwa-y_e_h
lunch	обяд	ob_ya_t
maid	камериерка	kameri-_e_rka
manager	управител	oopr_a_vitel

motel	мотел	*motel*
receipt	квитанция	*kvitantsi-ya*
reception	рецепция	*retseptsi-ya*
receptionist *(man)*	администратор	*administrator*
(woman)	администраторка	*administratorka*
restaurant	ресторант	*restorant*
room	стая	*sti-a*
room service	румсервиз	*roomservis*
shower	душ	*doosh*
single bed	единично легло	*edinichno leglo*
single room	единична стая	*ednichna sti-a*
toilet	тоалетна	*to-aletna*
twin room	стая с две легла	*sti-a zdveh legla*
washbasin	мивка	*mifka*

Have you any vacancies?
Имате ли свободни стаи?
imateh li svobodni sti?

I have a reservation
Имам резервация
imam rezervatsi-ya

I'd like a double/twin room
Моля, дайте ми двойна стая/стая с две легла
molya, diteh mi dvoyna sti-a/sti-a zdveh legla

I'd like a room with a bathroom/with a balcony
Моля, дайте ми стая с баня/с балкон
molya, diteh mi sti-a zbanya/zbalkon

I'd like a room for one night/three nights
Моля, дайте ми стая за една нощувка/три нощувки
molya, diteh mi sti-a za edna noshtoofka/tri noshtoofki

What is the charge per night?
Колко струва една нощувка?
kolko stroova edna noshtoofka?

I don't know yet how long I'll stay
Още не знам колко дълго ще остана
oshteh neh znam kolko dulgo shteh ostana

When is breakfast/dinner?
Кога е закуската/вечерята?
koga eh zakooskata/vecheryata?

Would you have my luggage brought up?
Бихте ли изпратили багажа ми в стаята?
biHteh li ispratili bagazha mi fstI-ata?

Please wake me at 7 o'clock
Моля, събудете ме в седем часа
molya, suboodeteh meh fsedem chasa

Can I have breakfast in my room?
Мога ли да поръчам закуска в стаята?
moga li da porucham zakooska fstI-ata?

I'll be back at 10 o'clock
Ще се върна в десет часа
shteh seh vurna vdeset chasa

My room number is 205
Номерът на стаята ми е двеста и пет
nomera na stI-ata mi eh dvesta i pet

I need a light bulb
Моля, сменете ми крушката
molya, smeneteh mi krooshkata

The lamp is broken
Лампата не работи
lampata neh raboti

There is no toilet paper in the bathroom
В банята няма тоалетна хартия
vbanyata nyama to-aletna Harti-ya

The window won't open
Прозорецът не се отваря
prozoretsa neh seh otvarya

The lift/shower isn't working
Асансьорът/душът не работи
asansyora/doosha neh raboti

There isn't any hot water
Няма топла вода
nyama topla voda

I'd like to have some laundry done *(said by a man/woman)*
Бих искал/искала да оставя дрехи за пране
biH iskal/iskala da ostavya dreHi za praneh

The socket in the bathroom doesn't work
Контактът в банята не работи
kontakta vbanyata neh raboti

I'm leaving tomorrow
Аз заминавам утре
as zaminavam ootreh

When do I have to vacate the room?
Кога трябва да освободя стаята?
koga tryabva da osvobodya stI-ata?

Can I have the bill please?
Моля, дайте ми сметката
molya, dIteh mi smetkata

Can I pay by credit card?
Мога ли да платя с кредитна карта
moga li da platya skreditna karta

I'll pay cash
Ще платя в брой
shteh platya vbroy

Can you get me a taxi?
Бихте ли ми поръчали такси?
biHteh li mi poruchali taxi?

Can you recommend another hotel?
Бихте ли ми препоръчали друг хотел?
biHteh li mi preporuchali drook Hotel?

THINGS YOU'LL SEE

аварien изход	*avari-en isHot*	emergency exit
асансьор	*asansyor*	lift
Балкантурист	*balkantoorist*	Balkantourist
баня	*banya*	bathroom
бутни	*bootni*	push
вана	*vana*	bath
втори етаж	*ftori etash*	second floor
вход	*fHot*	entrance
двойна стая	*dvoyna stI-a*	double room
добавка	*dobafka*	supplement
дръпни	*drupni*	pull
душ	*doosh*	shower
гараж	*garash*	garage
единична стая	*edinichna stI-a*	single room
закуска	*zakooska*	breakfast
Интерхотел	*interHotel*	Interhotel
мотел	*motel*	motel
нощувка и закуска	*noshtoofka i zakooska*	bed and breakfast
няма свободни легла/стаи	*nyama svobodni legla/stI*	no vacancies
обяд	*obyat*	lunch
офис	*ofis*	private
паркинг	*parkink*	car park
партер	*parter*	ground floor
персонал	*personal*	staff only
полупансион	*poloopansi-on*	half board

→

пълен пансион	*pulen pansi-on*	full board
първи етаж	*purvi etash*	first floor
резервация	*rezervatsi-ya*	reservation
ресторант	*restorant*	restaurant
рецепция	*retseptsi-ya*	reception
само за гости на хотела	*samo za gosti na Hotela*	hotel patrons only
сметка	*smetka*	bill
стая пол наем	*stI-a pod na-em*	room to let
стая с две легла	*stI-a zdveh legla*	twin room
сутерен	*sooteren*	basement
тоалетна	*to-aletna*	toilet
частен пансион	*chasten pansi-on*	guesthouse

REPLIES YOU MAY BE GIVEN

suzhalyavam, no nyamameh svobodni legla
I'm sorry, we're full

nyamameh svobodni edinichni/dvoyni stI
There are no single/double rooms left

za kolko noshti?
For how many nights?

kak biHteh zhelali da platiteh?
How will you be paying?

molya, plateteh predvaritelno
Please pay in advance

neh pri-emameh kreditni karti
We don't accept credit cards

tryabva da osvoboditeh stI-ata do dvanIset chasa
You must vacate the room by midday

CAMPING AND CARAVANNING

There are many campsites and caravan sites in Bulgaria and they are relatively evenly distributed over the whole country with a number of them along the coast. Conditions and type of accommodation vary – from space on a lawn for a tent or a caravan to the virtually hotel-like conditions of luxury tents or bungalows. All campsites and caravan sites have toilets, showers (there may be restrictions on the hot water availability) and kitchens or places for building a fire. Most sites will have a small grocer's shop or a kiosk for basic items and many will have at least a few market stalls where local people sell seasonal fruit and vegetables. Camping hardware like gas bottles, batteries etc, however, is extremely unlikely to be found for sale anywhere near the campsite – therefore buy all the hardware you need before you reach the site. Virtually all campsites and caravan sites close at the end of the summer. Camping rough and building fires in unauthorised places is illegal in Bulgaria and punishable by an on-the-spot fine. Campsites are indicated on most Bulgarian road maps.

There are no specifically designated youth hostels in Bulgaria but during the summer holidays some of the halls of residence студентско общежитие (*stoodentsko opshtezhiti-eh*) are used as youth hostels. You may be asked for an international student card before you are allocated a room. Places without student campuses may have basic accommodation in tourist dormitories туристическа спалня (*tooristicheska spalnya*) where you will be given a bunk in a large room sleeping 15-20 people. Mountain chalets offer a similar type of accommodation but a reservation from the Pirin Travel Agency in Sofia may be necessary.

USEFUL WORDS AND PHRASES

bucket	кофа	*kofa*
campfire	лагерен огън	*lageren ogun*
campsite	къмпинг	*kumpink*

26

caravan	караван	*karavan*
caravan site	къмпинг за каравани	*kumpink za karavani*
chalet	хижа	*Hizha*
cooking utensils	готварски пособия	*gotvarski posobi-ya*
cutlery	прибори за хранене	*pribori za Hraneneh*
drinking water	вода за пиене	*voda za pi-eneh*
hall of residence	студентско общежитие	*stoodentsko opshtezhiti-eh*
hitchhike	пътувам на автостоп	*putoovam na aftostop*
rope	въже	*vuzheh*
rubbish	отпадъци, боклук	*otpadutsi, boklook*
rucksack	раница	*ranitsa*
saucepans	тенджери	*tenjeri*
shop	магазин	*magazin*
sleeping bag	спален чувал	*spalen chooval*
tent	палатка	*palatka*
torch	електрическо фенерче	*elektrichesko fenercheh*
tourist dormitory	туристическа спалня	*tooristicheska spalnya*
trailer	ремарке	*remarkeh*

Can I camp here?
Мога ли да опъна палатка тук?
moga li da opuna palatka took?

Can we park the caravan here?
Можем ли да паркираме каравана тук?
mozhem li da parkirameh karavana took?

Where is the nearest campsite/caravan site?
Къде е най-близкия къмпинг/къмпинг за каравани?
kadeh eh nI-bliski-ya kumpink/kumpink za karavani?

What is the charge per night?
Колко струва на вечер?
kolko stroova na vecher?

I only want to stay for one night
Искам само да пренощувам
iskam samo da prenoshtoovam

Where is the kitchen?
Къде е кухнята?
kudeh eh kooHnyata?

Can I light a fire here?
Може ли да запаля огън тук?
mozheh li da zapalya ogun took?

Where can I get ...?
Къде мога да намеря ...?
kudeh moga da namerya ...?

Is there any drinking water?
Има ли вода за пиене?
ima li voda za pi-eneh?

THINGS YOU'LL SEE

вода за пиене	*voda za pi-eneh*	drinking water
душ	*doosh*	shower
забранено	*zabraneno*	forbidden
карта	*karta*	pass, identity card
кухня	*kooHnya*	kitchen
къмпинг	*kumpink*	campsite
огън	*ogun*	fire
опъването на палатки забранено	*opuvaneto na palatki zabraneno*	no camping
пропуск	*propoosk*	pass, identity card
студентско общежитие	*stoodentsko obshtezhiti-eh*	hall of residence
тоалетна	*to-aletna*	toilet
туристическа спалня	*tooristicheska spalnya*	tourist dormitory
цени	*tseni*	charges, tariff

MOTORING

In the seventies the Bulgarian government launched an ambitious building programme designed to link the major cities – Sofia, Plovdiv, Bourgas and Varna – with a circle of motorways (named *Traki-ya*, *Hemoos* and *Cherno Moreh*) which would serve as the backbone of the road system in the country. Dogged by continuous cash crises, the project is still incomplete although considerable parts of it have been built, notably the full length of the Sofia-Plovdiv motorway, plus an extension covering most of the way from Plovdiv to the Turkish border in the direction of Istanbul. The Sofia-Varna motorway, about a quarter of which is presently completed, covers the approaches to both cities. However, the country is adequately served by a good network of A-roads (often with a third lane on the busiest stretches of road).

Rules of the Road: drive on the right, overtake on the left. There are priority signs, but in the absence of these all secondary roads give way to major routes at junctions and crossroads. In the case of roads having equal status or at unmarked junctions, the traffic coming from the right has priority. Note that in Sofia, trams coming from any direction have priority. Roundabouts are almost unknown in Bulgaria; all traffic is regulated by lights but these are generally more visible than the ones in Britain – with three sets employed on bigger city junctions – an eye-level set for the first driver in a queue, a roadside set for medium-range visibility and an overhead set for long-range visibility. You must not overtake a tram that has stopped to allow passengers to get off. Both international and foreign driving licences are recognized. Civil liability insurance is compulsory and may be obtained at the border. The green and blue insurance cards are valid. The current law does not allow for any amount of alcohol in the blood, so do not drink and drive.

The speed limit on motorways is 120 km/h (75 mph) and on other main roads 80 km/h (50 mph), otherwise keep to the speed shown. In built-up areas the limit is 60 km/h (37 mph). A first-aid kit and a red warning triangle in case of breakdown or accidents must be carried at all times. Seat belts are compulsory.

Some petrol stations on main routes and in the cities are open 24 hours a day, but elsewhere they close late at night. Allow for at least 40 km between petrol stations and possibly more, since some of them have recently been closed; queuing may sometimes be necessary. Unleaded petrol is available along major routes and in most cities.

Fuel ratings are as follows:

normal (86 octane) – обикновен (*obiknoven*)
super (96 octane) – супер (*sooper*)
diesel – дизелово гориво (*dizelovo gorivo*)
unleaded – безоловен (*bezoloven*)

SOME COMMON ROAD SIGNS

автомагистрала	*aftomagistrala*	motorway
автоподлез	*aftopodles*	subway
включи фаровете	*fklyoochi faroveteh*	headlights on
влизането забранено	*vlizaneto zabraneno*	no entry, no tresspassing
внимание!	*vnimani-eh*	caution
внимание влак	*vnimani-eh vlak*	beware of the trains
внимание животни	*vnimani-eh zhivotni*	cattle crossing
внимание пешеходци	*vnimani-eh peshehottsi*	pedestrians
гараж	*garash*	garage
гараж! не паркирай!	*garash neh parkirı*	garage – no parking
еднопосочно движение	*ednoposochno dvizheni-eh*	one-way street
ж.п. прелез	*zheh peh preles*	level crossing
ж.п. преход	*zheh peh preHot*	beware of the trains
изпреварването забранено	*isprevarvaneto zabraneno*	no overtaking

→

карай бавно	*karI bavno*	slow
край на магистралата	*krI na magistralata*	end of motorway
кръстовище	*krustovishteh*	crossroads
лоша пътна настилка	*losha putna nastilka*	bad surface
митница	*mitnitsa*	customs
опасен завой	*opasen zavoy*	dangerous bend
опасен кръстопът	*opasen krustoput*	dangerous junction
опасност	*opasnost*	danger
отклонение	*otkloneni-eh*	diversion
паркинг	*parkink*	car park
пешеходна зона	*peshehodna zona*	pedestrian precinct
първа помощ	*purva pomosht*	first aid
път с предимство	*put spredimstvo*	give way
ремонт на пътя	*remont naputya*	roadworks
сервиз	*servis*	service station
училище	*oochilishteh*	school
център	*tsentur*	town centre

USEFUL WORDS AND PHRASES

boot	багажник	*bagazhnik*
brake *(noun)*	спирачка	*spirachka*
breakdown	повреда	*povreda*
car	лека кола	*leka kola*
caravan	караван	*karavan*
clutch	амбреаж	*ambreh-ash*
crossroads	кръстовище	*krustovishteh*
engine	двигател	*dvigatel*
exhaust	ауспух	*owspooH*
fanbelt	ремък	*remuk*
garage *(for repairs)*	сервиз	*servis*
(for petrol)	бензиностанция	*benzinostantsi-ya*
gear	скорост	*skorost*
gears	зъбни предавки	*zubni predafki*

31

headlights	фарове	*faroveh*
junction *(on motorway)*	магистрален възел	*magistralen vuzel*
licence	шофьорска книжка	*shofyorska knishka*
lorry	камион	*kami-on*
mirror	огледало	*ogledalo*
motorbike	мотоциклет	*mototsiklet*
motorway	автомагистрала	*aftomagistrala*
number plate	регистрационен номер	*registratsi-onen nomer*
petrol	бензин	*benzin*
rear lights	стопове	*stopoveh*
road	път	*put*
skid *(verb)*	занася се	*zanasya seh*
spares	резервни части	*rezervni chasti*
speed *(noun)*	скорост	*skorost*
speed limit	ограничение на скоростта	*ogranicheni-eh na skorosta*
speedometer	спидометър	*spidometur*
steering wheel	кормило	*kormilo*
tow	тегля	*teglya*
traffic jam	задръстване на движението	*zadrustvaneh na dvizheni-eto*
traffic lights	светофар	*svetofar*
trailer	ремарке	*remarkeh*
tyre	гума	*gooma*
van	камионетка	*kami-onetka*
wheel	колело	*kolelo*
windscreen	предно стъкло	*predno stuklo*
windscreen wiper	стъклочистачка	*stuklochistachka*

I'd like some petrol/oil/water
Дайте ми бензин/масло/вода
dIteh mi benzin/maslo/voda

Fill her up please!
Моля, напълнете резервоара!
molya, napulneteh rezerv-wara!

I'd like 35 litres of petrol
Дайте ми трийсет и пет литра бензин
dIteh mi treeset i pet litra benzin

Would you check the tyres please?
Бихте ли проверили гумите?
biHteh li proverili goomiteh?

Do you do repairs?
Правите ли авторемонти?
praviteh li aftoremonti?

Can you repair the clutch?
Можете ли да ремонтирате съединителната кутия?
mozheteh li da remontirateh suh-edinitelnata kooti-ya?

How long will it take?
Колко време ще отнеме?
kolko vremeh shteh otnemeh?

Where can I park?
Къде мога да паркирам?
kudeh moga da parkiram?

Can I park here?
Мога ли да паркирам тук?
moga li da parkiram took?

There is something wrong with the engine
Има повреда в двигателя
ima povreda v dvigatelya

The engine is overheating
Двигателят загрява
dvigatelya zagryava

I need a new tyre
Трябва ми нова гума
tryabva mi nova gooma

I'd like to hire a car
Искам да наема кола
iskam da na-ema kola

I'd like an automatic/a manual (said by a man/woman)
Бих искал/искала автоматичен модел/модел с ръчни скорости
biH iskal/iskala afttomatichen model/model sruchni skorosti

Is there a mileage charge?
Има ли такса на километър?
ima li taksa na kilometur?

Where is the nearest garage?
Къде е най-близкият сервиз?
kudeh eh nl-bliski-ya servis?

How do I get to Boyana?
Как да отида до Бояна?
kak da otida do bo-yana?

Is this the road to Veliko Turnovo?
Това ли е пътят за Велико Търново?
tova li eh putya za veliko turnovo?

DIRECTIONS YOU MAY BE GIVEN

ftorata flyavo	second on the left
nadyasno	on the right
nalyavo	on the left
napravo	straight on
pokrl ...	past the ...
purvata vdyasno	first on the right
zaveeteh nadyasno	turn right
zaveeteh nalyavo	turn left

THINGS YOU'LL SEE

безоловен бензин	*bezoloven benzin*	unleaded
бензин	*benzin*	petrol
бензиностанция	*benzinostantsi-ya*	petrol station
въздушно налягане	*vazdooshno nalyaganeh*	air pressure
дизелово гориво	*dizelovo gorivo*	diesel
глоба	*globa*	fine
изход	*isHot*	exit
колона	*kolona*	queue
масло	*maslo*	oil
налягане на гумите	*nalyaganeh na goomiteh*	tyre pressure
ниво на маслото	*nivo na masloto*	oil level
обикновен	*obiknoven*	86-octane petrol
отбивка	*otbifka*	diversion
ремонт	*remont*	repairs
сервиз	*servis*	garage for repairs
спирачна течност	*spirachna technost*	brake fluid
супер	*sooper*	96-octane petrol

THINGS YOU'LL HEAR

aftomatichen ili ruchen model iskateh?
Would you like an automatic or a manual?

diteh mi shofyorskata si knishka
May I see your licence?

molya, dokoomentiteh
Please show me your documents

TRAVELLING AROUND

AIR TRAVEL

No British airline currently provides services between the UK and Bulgarian destinations. The Bulgarian airline Balkan operates scheduled flights between Heathrow and Sofia four times a week; at busy times like Christmas you might find other European airlines offering flights between London and Sofia (eg Austrian Airlines). During most of the year (apart from April and November when there is a break), Balkan operates charter flights from most British airports to Varna/Bourgas on the Black Sea coast in the summer and to Sofia/Plovdiv in the winter. Flight-only deals on the charter flights to Bulgaria are hard to come by and are hardly ever advertised by travel agents; however, sometimes the price of a package holiday can be less than the price of the scheduled flight. There is also a domestic network connecting the capital with the main Bulgarian cities along the Danube and the Black Sea coast. From Sofia, Balkan operates very competitively priced scheduled routes to most Middle Eastern and North African capitals as well as to some Asian cities.

Visas are required for most foreign visitors but not for those arriving on package holidays.

RAIL TRAVEL

Most towns and villages in Bulgaria are connected by the Bulgarian State Railways, initials **БДЖ**. The majority of Bulgarian trains may not be particularly fast or comfortable but they are reliable and inexpensive. Most carriages are second class, but one or two per train will have first class seats. Every main town in the country is connected to the capital by at least one express service **експресен влак** (*expresen vlak*) a day; most lines are serviced by a so-called fast train **бърз влак** (*burs vlak*) which is marginally slower and is supposed to stop only at larger-than-average stations. Small villages and branch lines are served only by the excruciatingly slow local trains пътнически влак (*putnicheski vlak*). Long-distance overnight trains between the major cities have between one and three sleeper or couchette carriages (three- or six-berth compartments). Seats and berths should be reserved beforehand — ask for a reservation запазено място (*zapazeno myasto*). However, places on sleepers can also be bought from the sleeping car attendant on the night of travel. Larger cities may also have a Railway Bureau ж.п. бюро (*zheh peh byooro*), usually situated in the city centre, where you can buy tickets. Supplements and sometimes fines may be payable to the conductor on board if you take a faster train than stated on your ticket or wish to upgrade the class of your seat or berth.

LONG-DISTANCE BUS TRAVEL

Even the tiniest village in Bulgaria can be reached by bus from the local centre which in turn will be served by buses to several of the major cities. Most towns have bus stations автогара (*aftogara*) where tickets are sold until about half an hour before departure. The state-owned bus company Автотранспорт (*aftotransport*) runs dilapidated and noisy buses to most destinations; tickets for these do, however, have the advantage of being sold at rock-bottom prices. Privately-owned travel agents in bigger cities operate tourist-quality coach services to Sofia, Istanbul and other destinations. Cross-border coach travel may be subjected to very long delays on the border crossings to Turkey and Romania.

LOCAL TRANSPORT

Bulgarian cities have good bus networks. Tickets for all state-run services (which are the majority) should be purchased in advance at one of the many kiosks and newsstands in the streets; they cost a few leva each and can be used for three types of transport (bus, tram and trolleybus) anywhere in the country; it is practical therefore to buy several at a time. The passenger must validate his/her ticket by punching it in the machine on board the bus, tram or trolleybus. However, due to the recent increase in fare-dodging, some cities (like Varna) have reintroduced a conductor service. Many routes in the cities are served by privately operated minibus services with unspecified timetables (but they are fairly frequent during most of the day). On these the fare is paid to the driver.

TAXIS

The state-run taxi companies which until a few years ago had a monopoly on the trade and were very hard to come by, are now competing with countless private taxis. All taxis display the sign ТАКСИ. Most of the private taxis do not have meters and it would be wise to negotiate a price beforehand.

USEFUL WORDS AND PHRASES

adult	възрастен	*vuzrasten*
airport	летище	*letishteh*
airport bus	автобус до летището	*aftoboos do letishteto*
aisle seat	място до пътеката	*myasto do putekata*
baggage claim	получаване на багажа	*poloochavaneh na bagazha*
boarding card	бордна карта	*bordna karta*
boat	кораб	*korap*
booking office	бюро за билети	*byooro za bileti*
buffet	бюфет	*byoofet*
bus	автобус	*aftoboos*
bus station	автогара	*aftogara*
bus stop	автобусна спирка	*aftoboosna spirka*
carriage	вагон	*vagon*
check-in desk	регистрация на багажа	*registratsi-ya na bagazha*
child	дете	*deteh*
coach *(bus)*	автобус	*aftoboos*

compartment	купе	*koopeh*
connection	връзка	*vruska*
cruise	пътуване по море, круиз	*putoovaneh po moreh, kroo-is*
Customs	митница	*mitnitsa*
departure lounge	зала заминаване	*zala zaminavaneh*
domestic	вътрешен	*vutreshen*
domestic arrivals	пристигане вътрешни линии	*pristiganeh vutreshni linee*
domestic departures	заминаване вътрешни линии	*zaminavaneh vutreshni linee*
emergency exit	авариен изход	*avari-en isHot*
entrance	вход	*fHot*
exit	изход	*isHot*
fare	цена на билета	*tsena na bileta*
ferry	ферибот	*feribot*
first class	първа класа	*purva klasa*
flight	полет	*polet*
flight number	полет номер	*polet nomer*
gate	изход	*isHot*
hand luggage	ръчен багаж	*ruchen bagash*
international	международен	*mezhdoonaroden*
international arrivals	пристигане международни линии	*pristiganeh mezhdoonarodni linee*
international departures	заминаване международни линии	*zaminavaneh mezhdoonarodni linee*
left-luggage office	гардероб	*garderop*
lost property office	бюро изгубени вещи	*byooro izgoobeni veshti*
luggage trolley	количка за багаж	*kolichka za bagash*
minibus	микробус	*mikroboos*
non-smoking	непушачи	*nepooshachi*
number 5 bus	автобус номер пет	*aftoboos nomer pet*
passport	паспорт	*pasport*

platform	перон, коловоз	*peron, kolovos*
port	пристанище	*pristanishteh*
quay	кей	*kay*
railway	ж.п. линия	*zheh peh lini-ya*
reserved seat	запазено място	*zapazeno myasto*
restaurant car	вагон-ресторант	*vagon-restorant*
return ticket	билет за отиване и връщане	*bilet za otivaneh i vrushtaneh*
seat	място	*myasto*
second class	втора класа	*ftora klasa*
ship	кораб	*korap*
subway	подлез	*podles*
single ticket	билет	*bilet*
sleeper	спален вагон	*spalen vagon*
smoking	пушачи	*pooshachi*
station	гара	*gara*
taxi	такси	*taxi*
terminus (*bus*)	автогара	*aftogara*
ticket	билет	*bilet*
timetable	разписание	*raspisani-eh*
train	влак	*vlak*
tram	трамвай	*tramvl*
trolleybus	тролейбус	*trolayboos*
visa	виза	*viza*
waiting room	чакалня	*chakalnya*
window seat	място до прозореца	*myasto do prozoretsa*

AIR TRAVEL

I'd like a non-smoking seat please
Място за непушачи, моля
myasto za nepooshachi, molya

I'd like a window seat please
Място до прозореца, моля
myasto do prozoretsa, molya

How long will the flight be delayed?
Колко ще закъснее излитането?
kolko shteh zakusneh-yeh izlitaneto?

Which gate for the flight to London?
Кой е изходът за полета до Лондон?
koy eh isHoda za poleta do London?

RAIL, BUS AND LOCAL TRANSPORT

When does the train/bus for Sofia leave?
Кога заминава влакът/автобусът за София?
koga zaminava vlaka/aftoboosa za sofia?

When does the train/bus from Varna arrive?
Кога пристига влакът/автобусът от Варна?
koga pristiga vlaka/aftoboosa ot varna?

When is the next train/bus to Plovdiv?
Кога е следващият влак/автобус за Пловдив?
koga eh sledvashti-ya vlak/aftoboos za plovdif?

When is the first train/bus to Ruse?
Кога е първият влак/автобус за Русе?
koga eh purvi-ya vlak/aftoboos za rooseh?

When is the last train/bus to Burgas?
Кога е последният влак/автобус за Бургас?
koga eh posledni-ya vlak/aftoboos za boorgas?

What is the fare to Istanbul?
Колко струва билетът до Истанбул?
kolko stroova bileta do istanbool?

Do I have to change?
Ще трябва ли да сменям?
shteh tryabva li da smenyam?

Does the train/bus stop at Gabrovo?
Влакът/автобусът спира ли в Габрово?
vlaka/aftoboosa spira li v gabrovo?

How long does it take to get to Veliko Turnovo?
Колко време се пътува до Велико Търново?
kolko vremeh seh patoova do veliko turnovo?

Where can I buy a ticket?
Къде мога да си купя билет?
kudeh moga da si koopya bilet?

A single (ticket) to Sofia please
Един билет до София, моля
edin bilet do sofia, molya

A return ticket to Plovdiv please
Билет за отиване и връщане до Пловдив, моля
bilet za otivaneh i vrushtaneh do plovdif, molya

Could you help me get a ticket?
Бихте ли ми помогнали да си купя билет?
biHteh li mi pomognali da si koopya bilet?

Do I have to pay a supplement?
Трябва ли да платя добавка?
tryabva li da platya dobafka?

I'd like to reserve a seat
Със запазено място, моля
sus zapazeno myasto, molya

Is this the right train/bus for Vidin?
Това ли е влакът/автобусът за Видин?
tova li eh vlaka/aftoboosa za vidin?

Is this the right platform for the Pleven train?
На този коловоз ли е влака за Плевен?
na tozi kolovoz li eh vlaka za pleven?

Which platform for the Sliven train?
На кой коловоз е влакът за Сливен?
na koy kolovos eh vlaka za sliven?

Is the train/bus late?
Влакът/автобусът има ли закъснение?
vlaka/aftoboosa ima li zakasneni-eh?

Could you help me with my luggage please?
Извинете, бихте ли ми помогнали с багажа?
izvineteh, biHteh li mi pomognali zbagazha?

Is this a non-smoking compartment?
Това купе за непушачи ли е?
tova koopeh za nepooshachi li eh?

Is this seat free?
Свободно ли е това място?
svobodno li eh tova myasto?

This seat is taken
Това място е заето
tova myasto eh za-eto

I have reserved this seat
Това е моето запазено място
tova eh mo-eto zapazeno myasto

May I open/close the window?
Може ли да отворя/затворя прозореца?
mozheh li da otvorya/zatvorya prozoretsa?

When do we arrive in Kazanluk?
Кога пристигаме в Казанлък?
koga pristigameh fkazanluk?

What station is this?
Коя е тази гара?
ko-ya eh tazi gara?

Do we stop at Kaprivshtitsa?
Влакът спира ли в Копривщица?
vlaka spira li v koprifshtitsa?

Would you keep an eye on my things for a moment?
Извинете, бихте ли наглеждали багажа ми за минута?
izvineteh, biHteh li naglezhdali bagazha mi za minoota?

Is there a restaurant car on this train?
Има ли вагон-ресторант във влака?
ima li vagon-restorant vuf vlaka?

Where is the bus station?
Къде е автогарата?
kudeh eh aftogarata?

Where is there a bus stop?
Къде има спирка?
kudeh ima spirka?

Which buses go to Nesebar?
Кои автобуси отиват до Несебър?
ko-i aftoboosi otivat do nesebur?

How often do the buses to Golden Sands run?
На колко време са автобусите до Златните Пясъци?
na kolko vremeh sa aftoboositeh do zlatniteh pyasutsi?

Will you let me know when we're there?
Бихте ли ми казали когато стигнем дотам?
biHteh li mi kazali kogato stignem dotam?

Do I have to get off yet?
Тук ли трябва да сляза?
took li tryabva da slyaza?

How do you get to Varna city centre?
Как се отива до центъра на Варна?
kak seh otiva do tsentura na varna?

Do you go near the city centre?
Минавате ли покрай центъра на града?
minavateh li pokrI tsentura na grada?

I want to go to the Rila Monastery
Искам да отида до Рилския манастир
iskam da otida do rIlski-ya manastIr

TAXI

Where can I get a taxi?
Къде мога да взема такси?
kudeh moga da vzema taxI?

To the airport, please
До летището, моля
do letIshteto, molya

I'll give you 150 leva
Ще ви дам сто и петдесет лева
shteh vi dam sto i pedeset leva

Please stop here
Спрете тук, моля
spreteh took, molya

I'd like a receipt please
Бихте ли ми дали квитанция?
bIHteh li mi dali kvitantsi-ya?

I would like you to wait here for me and take me back
Ще ви помоля да ме изчакате тук и да ме върнете обратно
shteh vi pomolya da meh ischakateh took idameh-vurneteh obratno

Keep the change
Задръжте рестото
zadrushteh restoto

THINGS YOU'LL SEE

авариен изход	*avari-en isHot*	emergency exit
аварийна сигнализация	*avareena signalizatsi-ya*	emergency cord
Автотранспорт	*aftotransport*	state-owned bus company
автобус за летището	*aftoboos za letishteto*	airport bus
Балкан	*balkan*	Bulgarian Airlines
БДЖ	*beh-deh-zheh*	Bulgarian State Railways
билети	*bileti*	tickets, ticket office
билетна каса	*biletna kasa*	ticket office
бърз влак	*burz vlak*	fast train
бюро за билети	*byooro za bileti*	booking office
вагон	*vagon*	carriage
вход	*fHot*	entrance
вход забранен	*fHot zabranen*	no entry
вход от другата страна	*fHot ot droogata strana*	enter from the other side
възрастни	*vuzrastni*	adults
вътрешни линии	*vutreshni linee*	domestic (flights)
гардероб	*garderop*	left-luggage office
деца	*detsa*	children
директен полет	*direkten polet*	direct flight
добавка	*dobafka*	supplement
експресен влак	*ekspresen vlak*	express train
жени	*zheni*	ladies
ж.п. бюро	*zheh peh byooro*	Railway Bureau
заето	*za-eto*	engaged
закуски	*zakooski*	snacks
закъснение	*zakusneni-eh*	delay
заминаване	*zaminavaneh*	departures
запазено място	*zapazeno myasto*	reserved seat
изход	*isHot*	exit, gate
изход към пероните	*isHot kum peroniteh*	to the trains

→

46

информация	*informatsi-ya*	information
маршрут	*marshroot*	route
международни линии	*mezhdoonarodni linee*	international (flights)
места	*mesta*	seats
местно време	*mestno vremeh*	local time
митнически контрол	*mitnicheski kontrol*	customs control
мъже	*muzheh*	gents
нарушителите се глобяват	*narooshiteliteh seh globyavat*	penalty for misuse
не говорете с водача	*neh govoreteh zvodacha*	do not speak to the driver
неделя и почивни дни	*nedelya i pochivni dni*	Sundays and public holidays
непушачи	*nepooshachi*	non-smoking
не се навеждай навън	*neh seh navezhdɪ navun*	do not lean out of the window
не спира в ...	*ne spira v ...*	does not stop in ...
обмяна на валута	*obmyana na valoota*	currency exchange
паспортен контрол	*pasporten kontrol*	passport control
перон	*peron*	platform
плащам	*plashtam*	to pay
полет	*polet*	flight
получаване на багажа	*poloochavaneh na bagazha*	baggage claim
пристанище	*pristanishteh*	harbour
пристигане	*pristiganeh*	arrivals
пушачи	*pooshachi*	smoking
пушенето забранено	*poosheneto zabraneno*	no smoking
пътнически влак	*putnicheski vlak*	local train
пътници	*putnitsi*	passengers
пътуване	*putoovaneh*	journey
разписание	*raspisani-eh*	timetable
регистрация	*registratsi-ya*	check-in

→

47

редовен полет	*redoven polet*	scheduled flight
РЕП	*rep*	newspaper kiosk
само в работни дни	*samo frabotni dni*	weekdays only
свободно	*svobodno*	vacant
смяна в ...	*smyana v ...*	change at ...
спален вагон	*spalen vagon*	sleeper
спирка	*spirka*	stop
станция за таксита	*stantsi-ya za taksita*	taxi rank
такси	*taksi*	taxi
тоалетна	*to-aletna*	toilet
централна гара	*tsentralna gara*	central station
чакалня	*chakalnya*	waiting room

REPLIES YOU MAY BE GIVEN

sledvashti-ya vlak zaminava v ...
The next train leaves at ...

smyana v ...
Change at ...

tryabva da platiteh dobafka
You must pay a supplement

nyama svobodni mesta za ...
There are no more seats available for ...

THINGS YOU'LL HEAR

imateh li bagash?
Do you have any luggage?

pooshachi ili nepooshachi?
Smoking or non-smoking?

→

myasto do prozoretsa ili do putekata?
Window seat or aisle seat?

molya pasporta/bileta
Can I see your passport/ticket, please?

purvo povikvaneh na putnitsiteh za ...
The flight for ... is now boarding

molya putnitsiteh za ... da seh nasochat kum isHot nomer ...
Would the passengers to ... go to gate number ...

vnimani-eh
Attention

molya biletiteh
Tickets please

kacheteh seh na vlaka
Board the train

vlakut za ... shteh zamineh ot ... kolovos v ... chasa
The train for ... will leave from platform ... at ...

vlak nomer ... shteh pristigneh na ... kolovos v ... chasa
Train number ... will arrive at platform ... at ...

vlak nomer ... seh dvizhi sus ... minooti zakusneni-eh
Train number ... is ... minutes late

vashi-ya pasport, molya
Your passport, please

molya otvoreteh koofariteh
Open your suitcases, please

imateh li neshto za deklariraneh?
Do you have anything to declare ?

RESTAURANTS

Like most of the hotels, the majority of restaurants (**ресторант** *restorant*) in Bulgaria used to be owned by the state-run tourist company Balkantourist. This has imposed a certain uniformity in design and choice of food. Although categories exist, they are not clearly indicated but can be easily guessed once you have had a look at the place. Restaurants are usually open between 11 am-2 pm and 6 pm-11 pm daily.

Waiter-service restaurants fall roughly into two kinds: 'international' and folk-style. Both types can offer high quality or mediocre food, although the majority will have something in between. Finding out about each place in particular is very much a matter of trial and error.

More specifically the kinds of eating places in Bulgaria are:
Waiter-service restaurants:
  – hotel and high street restaurants: good quality international cuisine, if slightly pricier than average;
  – **ханче** (*hancheh*) or **механа** (*meHana*): Bulgarian folk restaurants providing home-style cooking served in nineteenth century folk-style environment (waiters in national dress, etc).
Self-service restaurants:
  – **закусвалня** (*zakoosvalnya*) cafeteria: unlicensed and very cheap places but rarely very clean. They sell snacks as well as soups and hot dishes.
  – **скара-бира** (*skara-bira*) grill and beer joints: rough-and-ready shed-type affairs with tables outside where the burger-style meats are barbecued as you wait and are then traditionally washed down with Bulgarian beer. This fare is incidentally what Bulgarians excel in making and consuming. It is well worth trying if you want to find out about the flavour of local life.

Ethnic restaurants are mostly to be found in Sofia with some Chinese and Vietnamese, European and Mexican cooking represented, but don't be surprised if the dishes differ slightly from what you are used to as they will be made from mostly local ingredients.

In bigger cities and package resorts there are variety restaurants which stage entertainment of, for example, a Bulgarian wedding, gypsy and shepherd rituals, dancing on hot coals etc.

Drinking places have increased both in number and in variety since the end of the ban on private enterprise. Most of these are called **кафе-аперитиф** (*kafeh-aperitif*) and offer local and imported spirits, soft drinks and sometimes ice cream. They are usually waiter-service and the service can be slow. Smoking is allowed in all licensed establishments and ventilation is rarely good, so finding an outside table is always the best option. Older Bulgarians tend to use restaurants for social drinking; the younger drinkers prefer the *kafeh-aperitif* bars. Western-style bars exist in most hotels and are generally known as **дневен бар** (*dneven bar*) 'day-bar' (open 11 am-11 pm) as opposed to the **нощен бар** (*noshten bar*) 'night bar' or 'nightclub' establishments, mostly to be found in the more up-market hotels – these are are variety clubs with a floor show and are open between 10 pm and 4 am.

Another popular catering establishment often seen in Bulgaria is the café-pâtisserie – **сладкарница** (*slatkarnitsa*). Its main fare is a selection of syrupy cakes and cream cakes, toasted sandwiches, ice creams and non-alcoholic hot and cold drinks. They are only licensed if they are in a hotel and double as day-bars.

Probably the best place to have breakfast in Bulgaria is one of the small street bakeries which churn out hot cheese-filled pastries, **баничка** (*banichka*), marmalade-filled sweet rolls, **кифла** (*kifla*), and bagels, **геврек** (*gevrek*), all day long. These bakeries do not sell anything else or have tables – the only option being to eat on the hoof, which is quite acceptable in Bulgaria.

USEFUL WORDS AND PHRASES

beer	бира	*bira*
bill	сметка	*smetka*
bottle	бутилка	*bootilka*
cake	паста	*pasta*
chef	майстор-готвач	*mistor-gotvach*
coffee	кафе	*kafeh*
cup	чаша	*chasha*

RESTAURANTS

fork	вилица	*vilitsa*
glass	чаша	*chasha*
knife	нож	*nosh*
menu	меню	*menyoo*
milk	мляко	*mlyako*
plate	чиния	*chini-ya*
receipt	касова бележка	*kasova beleshka*
sandwich	сандвич	*sandvich*
serviette	салфетка	*salfetka*
snack	закуска	*zakooska*
soup	супа	*soopa*
spoon	лъжица	*luzhitsa*
sugar	захар	*zaHar*
table	маса	*masa*
tea	чай	*chI*
teaspoon	лъжичка	*luzhichka*
tip	бакшиш	*bakshish*
waiter	сервитьор	*servityor*
waitress	сервитьорка	*servityorka*
water	вода	*voda*
wine	вино	*vino*
wine list	меню за напитки	*menyoo za napitki*

A table for one please
Маса за един, моля
masa za edin, molya

A table for two please
Маса за двама, моля
masa za dvama, molya

Can I see the menu?
Бихте ли ми дали менюто?
biHteh li mi dali menyooto?

Can I see the wine list?
Бихте ли ми дали менюто за напитки?
biHteh li mi dali menyooto za napitki?

What would you recommend?
Какво ще ми препоръчате?
kakvo shteh mi preporuchateh?

I'd like ...
Моля, дайте ми ...
molya, dIteh mi ...

Just a cup of coffee/tea, please
Само едно кафе/чай, моля
samo edno kafeh/chI, molya

Waiter/ waitress!
Моля!
molya!

Can we have the bill, please?
Моля, сметката!
molya, smetkata!

I only want a snack *(said by a man/woman)*
Бих искал/искала само лека закуска
biH iskal/iskala samo leka zakooska

I didn't order this
Аз не поръчах това
as neh poruchaH tova

May we have some more ...?
Бихте ли донесли още ...?
biHteh li donesli oshteh ...?

The meal was very good, thank you
Яденето беше чудесно, благодаря
yadeneto besheh choodesno, blagodarya

My compliments to the chef!
Благодарете на майстора от мое име!
blagodareteh na mIstora ot mo-eh imeh!

53

I think there is a mistake in the bill
Струва ми се, че има грешка в сметката
str<u>oo</u>va mi seh, cheh <u>i</u>ma gr<u>e</u>shka fsm<u>e</u>tkata

---

THINGS YOU MAY SEE

бирария	*birari-ya*	beer and grills joint, pub
гардероб	*garder<u>o</u>p*	cloakroom
гардеробът е задължителен	*garder<u>o</u>but eh zadulzh<u>i</u>telen*	cloakroom obligatory
каса	*k<u>a</u>sa*	pay here
кафе	*kaf<u>e</u>h*	coffee shop
кухня	*k<u>oo</u>Hnya*	kitchens
ресторант	*restor<u>a</u>nt*	restaurant
офис	*<u>o</u>fis*	kitchens
самообслужване	*samo-opsl<u>oo</u>zhivaneh*	self-service
тоалетна	*to-al<u>e</u>tna*	toilets

MENU READER

STARTERS

гъби с масло *gubi smaslo*	mushrooms fried in butter
език пане *ezik paneh*	fried tongue in batter
жабешки бутчета *zhabeshki bootcheta*	frogs' legs
картофи със сирене *kartofi sus sireneh*	chips with feta cheese
кашкавал *kashkaval*	hard yellow cheese
кашкавал пане *kashkaval paneh*	fried yellow cheese in batter
кьополу *kyopoloo*	chopped baked aubergines and peppers with tomatoes and garlic in vinaigrette
луканка *lookanka*	long, flat, dry-cured, spicy sausage, served in thin slices
маслини с лук *maslini slook*	olives with onion
миди *midi*	mussels
мозък пане *mozuk paneh*	fried brains in batter
омлет със сирене *omlet sus sireneh*	cheese omelette
омлет по градинарски *omlet po gradinarski*	vegetable omelette
охлюви *oHlyoovi*	snails
патладжан бюрек *patladjan byoorek*	fried aubergine stuffed with cheese paste
сирене *sireneh*	feta cheese
суджук *soojook*	horse-shoe shaped, dry-cured sausage, similar to *lookanka*
тиквичка бюрек *tikvichka byoorek*	fried courgette stuffed with cheese paste
тиквички пържени *tikvichki purzheni*	fried sliced courgettes
филе *fileh*	dry-cured, spicy pork or venison fillet, served in thin slices
хемендекс *hemendeks*	ham and eggs
червен хайвер *cherven HIver*	red caviar
черен хайвер *cheren HIver*	caviar
чушка бюрек *chooshka byoorek*	fried pepper stuffed with cheese paste and eggs
чушки пържени *chooshki purzheni*	fried peppers
шкембе в гювече *shkembeh vgyoovecheh*	tripe stew, made in an earthenware pot

55

шпеков салам *shpekof salam*   salami

SALADS

варен боб с лук *varen bop slook*   bean salad with onion
домати *domati*   tomatoes
домати със сирене *domati sus sireneh* tomatoes with feta cheese
зеле *zeleh*   raw, finely chopped cabbage
зелена салата *zelena salata*   salad of lettuce, spring onions
        and radishes
картофи с лук *kartofi slook*   potato salad with onion
краставици *krastavitsi*   cucumbers
мешана *meshana*   tomatoes and cucumbers
мешана с лук *meshana slook*   tomatoes, cucumbers and
        onion
руска *rooska*   Russian salad (potatoes, peas,
        ham, gherkins, boiled eggs –
        chopped and mixed with
        mayonnaise)
чушки *chooshki*   baked peppers served cold in
        vinaigrette
шопска *shopska*   tomatoes, cucumber, onion,
        peppers, parsley and feta
        cheese

SOUPS

градинарска чорба *gradinarska chorba* mixed vegetable soup
гулаш *goolash*   goulash soup – made with
        vegetables, pulses and paprika
крем-супа от домати *krem-soopa ot*   cream of tomato soup
  domati
курбан чорба *koorban chorba*   lamb soup with rice
манастирска чорба *manastirska chorba* white bean and vegetable soup
супа от спанак *soopa ot spanak*   spinach soup
супа от леща *soopa ot leshta*   lentil soup
супа топчета *soopa topcheta*   soup with meatballs
таратор *tarator*   cold soup made from chopped
        cucumber, yoghurt, garlic,
        dill and walnuts

| телешко варено *teleshko vareno* | veal and vegetables in clear bouillon |
| шкембе чорба *shkembeh chorba* | tripe soup |

MEAT DISHES

агнешка дроб-сарма *agneshka dropsarma*	spicy lamb and lamb offal roasted in caul parcels
винен кебап *vinen kebap*	pork stewed in wine
гювеч *gyoovech*	pork and vegetable stew baked in an earthenware dish called a *gyoovech*; contains peppers, tomatoes, onions, aubergines, okra, potatoes, parsley
дивеч *divech*	game
домашна наденица *domashna nadenitsa*	Bulgarian pork and beef sausage
задушено пиле *zadoosheno pileh*	chicken stewed with vegetables
карета *kareta*	grilled pork fillets
карначета *karnacheta*	thin, round, grilled Bulgarian sausage
кебапчета *kebapcheta*	grilled oblong rissoles
кюфтета *kyoofteta*	grilled meatballs
мешана скара *meshana skara*	mixed grill of pork fillet, *kebapcheh*, large meatball, pork on a skewer, round sausage and often mushrooms
мусака *moosaka*	moussaka — layers of minced meat, potatoes, aubergines and tomatoes, topped with a white sauce made with eggs
пиле на грил *pileh na gril*	grilled chicken
пълнени пиперки *pulneni piperki*	roast peppers stuffed with mince
пържен дроб *purzhen drop*	fried liver
пържола на тиган *purzhola na tigan*	fried pork chop
сарми *sarmi*	vine or cabbage leaves stuffed with mince
свинско каварма *svinsko kavarma*	diced pork stewed with onion

свинско с кисело зеле *svinsko skiselo zeleh* — pork stewed with sauerkraut

свинско филе вретено *svinsko fileh vreteno* — pork fillet rolled with ham, cheese and mushrooms

сирене по тракийски *sireneh po trakeeski* — feta cheese and *lookanka* baked in an earthenware pot

телешко филе с гъби *teleshko fileh zgubi* — tenderloin of veal with mushrooms

телешки гулаш *teleshki goolash* — beef goulash

филе с гъби *fileh zgubi* — pork fillet with mushrooms

шишчета *shishcheta* — lamb or pork shish kebabs

шницел *shnitsel* — breaded fried pork and beef burger

шницел натурален *shnitsel natooralen* — breaded cutlet or burger

FISH

акула *akoola* — shark

аншуа *anshoo-a* — anchovy fillets

бяла риба *byala riba* — pikeperch

есетра *esetra* — sturgeon

калкан *kalkan* — turbot

калмари *kalmari* — squid

кефал *kefal* — grey mullet

костур *kostoor* — perch

мерлуза *merlooza* — hake

миди *midi* — mussels

паламуд *palamoot* — tuna

попче *popcheh* — bullhead (similar to white fish)

пъстърва *pusturva* — trout

рак *rak* — crab, lobster

скариди *skaridi* — shrimps

скумрия *skoomri-ya* — mackerel

сом *som* — sheatfish (type of catfish)

хамсия *hamsi-ya* — sprat

цаца *tsatsa* — whitebait

чирози *chirozi* — dried salted fish

шаран *sharan* — carp

щука *shtooka* — pike

FISH DISHES

варени раци *vareni ratsi* boiled freshwater lobsters
варена риба *varena riba* boiled or poached fish
задушена риба *zadooshena riba* fish stewed with local herbs and spices
маринована риба *marinovana riba* fish pickled in marinade and spices
миди с ориз *midi soris* boiled mussels stewed with rice
паламуд *palamoot* steaks of dry-cured tuna
пълнена риба *pulnena riba* roast fish (usually carp) filled with nut stuffing
пържена риба *purzhena riba* fried fish (usually small fish)
риба на керемида *riba na keremida* fish roasted in a ceramic dish shaped like a roof tile
риба на скара *riba na skara* grilled fish (usually fillets of the larger varieties of fish)
риба на фурна *riba na foorna* oven-baked whole fish
риба плакия *riba plaki-ya* fish stewed with mixed vegetables
рибена чорба *ribena chorba* clear soup of small fish and vegetables
салата от чирози *salata ot chirozi* sun-dried fillets of fish in dill and vinegar
хайвер *HIver* taramasalata, caviar, fish roe

VEGETARIAN DISHES

вегетариански гювеч *vegetari-anski gyoovech* vegetable stew with cheese
имам баялдъ *imam ba-yalduh* aubergine, onion and tomato stew
картофи огретен *kartofi ogreten* potatoes baked with eggs and cheese
манастирски гювеч *manastirski gyoovech* mixed vegetable bake
омлет с пресен лук *omlet spresen look* baked eggs with spring onions and cheese
сирене на фурна *sireneh na foorna* feta cheese with paprika toasted in greaseproof paper
сирене по шопски *sireneh po shopski* feta cheese, tomato and egg, baked in an earthenware pot

59

спанак със сирене *spanak sus sireneh*
spinach stewed with eggs and
     cheese

тиквички пълнени със сирене
tikvichki pulneni sus sireneh
baked courgettes stuffed with
     feta cheese

чушки със сирене *chooshki sus sireneh*
eggs
baked peppers stuffed with
     and cheese

BREAD AND PASTRIES

баница *banitsa*
cheese and egg pastry

баница със спанак *banitsa sus spanak*
cheese, egg and spinach pastry

геврек *gevrek*
bagel

кифла *kifla*
sweet bread roll filled with
     marmalade

мекици *mekitsi*
deep-fried light dough
     sprinkled with caster sugar

милинки *milinki*
cheese buns

поничка *ponichka*
doughnut

сиренка *sirenka*
bread roll with cheese

тиквеник *tikvenik*
pumpkin pie

хляб *Hlyap*
bread

DESSERTS

ашуре *ashooreh*
boiled whole wheat with sugar
     and nuts

баклава *baklava*
baklava – flaky pastry with
     chopped nuts, soaked in
     syrup

грис-халва *gris halva*
moist semolina cake

еклер *ekler*
éclair

кадаиф *kada-if*
shredded pastry soaked in `
     syrup

кисело мляко *kiselo mlyako*
yoghurt

компот *kompot*
preserved fruit in syrup

крем *krem*
custard-style pudding

крем ванилия *krem vanili-ya*
vanilla custard

крем карамел *krem karamel*
crème caramel

крем шоколадов *krem shokoladof*
chocolate pudding

курабии *koorabee*
soft biscuits

локум *lokoom*
Turkish delight

юкум "Роза" *lok<u>oo</u>m r<u>o</u>za	Turkish delight with attar of roses
юкум с орехи *lok<u>oo</u>m s<u>o</u>reHi	Turkish delight with walnuts
малеби *maleb<u>i</u>	pudding flavoured with attar of roses and topped with syrup
мелба *m<u>e</u>lba	ice cream topped with biscuits, jam and nuts
мляко с ориз *ml<u>ya</u>ko sor<u>i</u>s	rice pudding
палачинка *palach<u>i</u>nka	pancake
палачинка с мед и орехи *palach<u>i</u>nka smet i-<u>o</u>reHi	pancake filled with honey and crushed walnuts
палачинка с конфитюр *palach<u>i</u>nka skonfit<u>yoo</u>r	pancake filled with jam
паста *p<u>a</u>sta	cake filled with butter cream
печена тиква *p<u>e</u>chena t<u>i</u>kva	baked pumpkin
саварина *savar<u>i</u>na	rum baba
сладко *sl<u>a</u>tko	jam
сладолед *sladol<u>e</u>t	ice cream
сладолед "Ескимо" *sladol<u>e</u>t esk<u>i</u>mo	ice cream on a stick, covered in chocolate
сладолед млечен *sladol<u>e</u>t ml<u>e</u>chen	low fat milk ice cream
сладолед плодов *sladol<u>e</u>t pl<u>o</u>dof	iced fruit juice
сладолед сметанов *sladol<u>e</u>t smet<u>a</u>nof	vanilla ice cream
сладолед шоколадов *sladol<u>e</u>t shokol<u>a</u>dof	chocolate ice cream
сметана *smet<u>a</u>na	cream
сметана разбита *smet<u>a</u>na razb<u>i</u>ta	whipped cream
торта *t<u>o</u>rta	cream cake with syrup
торта "Гараш" *t<u>o</u>rta g<u>a</u>rash	chocolate cake
торта плодова *t<u>o</u>rta pl<u>o</u>dova	cream cake with fresh fruit
тригуна *trig<u>oo</u>na	baklava with whipped cream
халва *halv<u>a</u>	halva – sweet made from sesame seed paste and syrup
целувки *tsel<u>oo</u>fki	meringue

61

FRUIT, NUTS AND SEEDS

ананас *anan<u>a</u>s*	pineapple
бадеми *bad<u>e</u>mi*	almonds
банани *ban<u>a</u>ni*	bananas
вишни *v<u>i</u>shni*	morello cherries
грозде *gr<u>o</u>zdeh*	grapes
диня *d<u>i</u>nya*	water melon
кайсии *kIs<u>ee</u>*	apricots
кашу *kash<u>oo</u>*	cashew
киви *k<u>i</u>vi*	kiwi
круши *kr<u>oo</u>shi*	pears
лимон *lim<u>o</u>n*	lemon
малини *mal<u>i</u>ni*	raspberries
мандарини *mandar<u>i</u>ni*	tangerines
орехи *<u>o</u>reHi*	walnuts
портокали *portok<u>a</u>li*	oranges
праскови *pr<u>a</u>skovi*	peaches
пъпеш *p<u>u</u>pesh*	melon
семки *s<u>e</u>mki*	sunflower seeds
сливи *sl<u>i</u>vi*	plums
смокини *smok<u>i</u>ni*	figs
фъстъци *fust<u>u</u>tsi*	peanuts
череши *cher<u>e</u>shi*	cherries
ябълки *<u>ya</u>bulki*	apples
ягоди *<u>ya</u>godi*	strawberries

VEGETABLES

боб *bop*	beans
грах *gr<u>a</u>H*	peas
гъби *g<u>u</u>bi*	mushrooms
домати *dom<u>a</u>ti*	tomatoes
зеле *z<u>e</u>leh*	cabbage
картофи *kart<u>o</u>fi*	potatoes
карфиол *karfi-<u>o</u>l*	cauliflower
копър *k<u>o</u>pur*	dill
краставица *kr<u>a</u>stavitsa*	cucumber
леща *l<u>e</u>shta*	lentils
лук *look*	onion
магданоз *magdan<u>o</u>s*	parsley

маруля *maroolya*	lettuce
моркови *morkovi*	carrots
ориз *oris*	rice
патладжан *patlajan*	aubergine
пържени картофи *purzheni kartofi*	chips
спанак *spanak*	spinach
тиквички *tikvichki*	courgettes, marrows
царевица *tsarevitsa*	sweet corn
чесън *chesun*	garlic
чушки *chooshki*	peppers

MISCELLANEOUS

варено *vareno*	boiled
горчица *gorchitsa*	mustard
задушено *zadoosheno*	braised
захар *zaHar*	sugar
захарин *zaHarin*	sweetener
кетчуп *ketchoop*	tomato ketchup
конфитюр *konfityoor*	jam
майонеза *mayoneza*	mayonnaise
маргарин *margarin*	margarine
масло *maslo*	butter
мед *met*	honey
на скара *naskara*	grilled
олио *olio*	vegetable oil
оцет *otset*	vinegar
печено *pecheno*	roast
пушено *poosheno*	smoked
пълнено *pulneno*	stuffed
пържено *purzheno*	fried
салам *salam*	sausage
сметана *smetana*	cream
сол *sol*	salt
сурово *soorovo*	raw
сушено *soosheno*	dried
чеверме *chevermeh*	barbecued on a spit
черен пипер *cheren piper*	black pepper
яйце *yItseh*	egg

SOFT DRINKS

айрян *Iryan*	cold diluted yoghurt drink
боза *boza*	very thick sweet drink made of barley and malt
вода *voda*	water
газирана вода *gazirana voda*	soda water
кафе *kafeh*	coffee
кафе еспресо *kafeh espreso*	espresso coffee
кафе капучино *kafeh kapoochino*	cappuccino
кафе с мляко *kafeh smlyako*	coffee with milk
кафе със сметана *kafeh sus smetana*	coffee with cream
кафе нес *kafeh nes*	instant coffee
лимонада *limonada*	lemonade
минерална вода *mineralna voda*	mineral water (still)
мляко *mlyako*	milk
нектар *nektar*	juice with fruit pulp
нектар от кайсии *nektar ot kIsee*	apricot *nektar*
нектар от праскови *nektar ot praskovi*	peach *nektar*
сок *sok*	fruit or fruit-flavoured juice
сок от ананас *sok ot ananas*	pineapple juice
сок от вишни *sok ot vishni*	morello cherry juice
сок от домати *sok ot domati*	tomato juice
сок от малини *sok ot malini*	raspberry juice
сок от портокали *sok ot portokali*	orange juice
сок от ябълки *sok ot yabulki*	apple juice
сок от ягоди *sok ot yagodi*	strawberry juice
тоник *tonik*	tonic
турско кафе *toorsko kafeh*	Turkish-style coffee (finely-ground coffee boiled in a small pot and served unfiltered)
чай *chI*	tea
чай английски *chI angleeski*	English-style tea
чай билков *chI bilkof*	mixed herbal tea
чай китайски *chI kitIski*	China tea (black or green)
чай липов *chI lipof*	lime flower tea
чай ментов *chI mentof*	peppermint tea
чай шипков *chI shipkof*	rosehip tea
топъл шоколад *topul shokolat*	hot chocolate

ALCOHOLIC DRINKS

бира *bira*	beer
бира "Астика" *bira astika*	⎫
бира "Галатея" *bira galateh-ya*	⎬ brands of luxury strong lager
бира "Загорка" *bira zagorka*	⎭
бира наливна *bira nalivna*	draught beer
бира "Светло пиво" *bira svetlo pivo*	lager
бира "Шуменско пиво" *bira shoomensko pivo*	a brand of luxury strong lager
вермут *vermoot*	vermouth
вино *vino*	wine
водка *votka*	vodka
джин *jin*	gin
коняк *konyak*	any good quality brandy
ликьор *likyor*	liqueur
мастика *mastika*	Bulgarian version of Greek ouzo
ракия *raki-ya*	Bulgarian traditional plum or grape brandy
шампанско *shampansko*	champagne or any sparkling wine
уиски *wiski*	whisky

DRINKS-RELATED TERMS

бяло *byalo*	white
газирано *gazirano*	sparkling, fizzy
десертно вино *desertno vino*	sweet wine
коктейл *koktayl*	cocktail
нискоалкохолно *niskoalkoHolno*	low-alcohol
полусухо *poloosooHo*	medium-dry
розе *rozeh*	pink
сухо *sooHo*	dry
червено *cherveno*	red

BULGARIAN WINES

RED

Гъмза *gumza*	heavy, mellow, full-bodied
Каберне *kaberne*	full-bodied

MENU READER

Мавруд *mavroot*	rich, dark, heavy, dry
Мелник *melnik*	very thick, heavy, mellow, full-bodied
Мерло *merlo*	with a hint of strawberry
Мускател *mooskatel*	sweet dessert wine
Памид *pamit*	sweet, verging on rosé
Пирин *pirin*	blend of *pamit* and *melnik*
Тракия *traki-ya*	blend of *pamit* and *mavroot*

WHITE

Димят *dimyat*	fine bouquet, very dry
Евксиноград *efksinograt*	by far the finest, dry and medium-dry varieties, rich bouquet
Карловски мискет *karlofski misket*	medium-dry, aromatic
Магарешко мляко *magareshko mlyako*	medium-dry, light
Тамянка *tamyanka*	medium-dry, light

SPARKLING

Искра *iskra*	both red and white available, medium-dry to sweet

MENU TERMS

българска национална кухня *bulgarska natsi-onalna kooHnya*	Bulgarian national cuisine
готвач *gotvach*	cook
десерт *desert*	dessert
майстор-готвач *mIstor gotvach*	chef
меню *menyoo*	menu
ордьовър *ordyovur*	hors d'œuvre
основно ястие *osnovno yasti-eh*	main course
половин порция *polovin portsi-ya*	half (child's) portion
порция *portsi-ya*	portion
сметка *smetka*	bill
специалитет *spetsi-alitet*	speciality dish

SHOPS AND SERVICES

Shops in Bulgaria are usually open Mondays to Fridays between 8 am and 5 pm, and on Saturdays between 9 am and 2 pm. It is quite common to find in quieter places that there is a statutory siesta time, in which case the opening times will be 8 am-12 pm and 3-7 pm. Supermarkets and department stores usually stay open until 8 pm, including Saturdays. In the larger cities there are food shops which are open round the clock.

Goods worth looking for include replicas of antique jewellery, leather accessories, woodcarvings, embroidery, metalwork and folk-music instruments – notably Bulgarian bagpipes, гайда (*gĺda*). The best samples of these are to be found in the specialised craft museums and ethnographical centres like Etura, near the town of Gabrovo, and in the shops of the Union of Bulgarian Artists, **Съюз на българските художници** (*suyoos na bulgarskiteh hoodozhnitsi*), and the Union of Bulgarian Traditional Craftsmen, **Задруга на майсторите на художествени занаяти** (*zadrooga na mĺstoriteh na hoodozhestveni zana-yati*). Good-quality copies of old Orthodox icons are on sale in art shops but can occasionally be bought at reasonable prices from street artists.

Other specifically Bulgarian items are yoghurt **кисело мляко** (*kiselo mlyako*) and rose-petal jam **сладко от рози** (*slatko ot rozi*). Bulgaria prides itself as the home of yoghurt and it is certainly the place where the bacteria *lactobacillus bulgaricus* (which makes the milk 'curdle' into yoghurt) grows best, as its name confirms.

Since the advent of AIDS shaving has been withdrawn from the range of services offered by men's hairdressers. Most ladies' hairdressers have a beauty parlour on their premises.

USEFUL WORDS AND PHRASES

bakery	фурна	*foorna*
bookshop	книжарница	*knizharnitsa*
butcher's	месарница	*mesarnitsa*
buy *(verb)*	купувам	*koopoovam*
cake shop	сладкарница	*slatkarnitsa*
cheap	евтин	*eftin*
chemist's	аптека	*apteka*
confectioner's	магазин за захарни изделия	*magazin za zaHarni izdeli-ya*
department store	универсален магазин	*ooniversalen magazin*
dry cleaner's	химическо чистене	*Himichesko chisteneh*
electrical goods	електрически уреди	*elektricheski ooredi*
fishmonger	рибарски магазин	*ribarski magazin*
florist's	цветарски магазин	*tsvetarski magazin*
greengrocer's	плод-зеленчук	*plodzelenchook*
grocer's	хранителни стоки	*Hranitelni stoki*
hairdresser's		
(men's)	бръснарски салон	*brusnarski salon*
(women's)	фризьорски салон	*frizyorski salon*
handicrafts shop	магазин за народни занаяти	*magazin za narodni zana-yati*
jeweller's	бижутерия	*bizhooteri-ya*
ladies' wear	дамска конфекция	*damska konfektsi-ya*
market	пазар	*pazar*
menswear	мъжка конфекция	*mushka konfektsi-ya*
newsagent's	РЕП	*rep*
receipt	касова бележка	*kasova beleshka*
record shop	музикален магазин	*moozikalen magazin*
sale	разпродажба	*rasprodazhba*
shoe repairer's	обущар	*obooshtar*
shoe shop	магазин за обувки	*magazin za oboofki*
shop	магазин	*magazin*
shop assistant		
(man)	продавач	*prodavach*
(woman)	продавачка	*prodavachka*

special offer	намалена цена	*namalena tsena*
spend	харча	*harcha*
stationer's	канцеларски пособия	*kantselarski posobi-ya*
tailor	шивач	*shivach*
till	каса	*kasa*
tobacconist's	магазин за цигари	*magazin za tsigari*
toyshop	магазин за играчки	*magazin za igrachki*
travel agent	туристическо бюро	*tooristichesko byooro*

Excuse me, where is/are ...?
Извинете, къде се намира/намират ...?
izvineteh, kudeh seh namira/namirat ...?

Where is there a ... shop?
Къде има магазин за ...?
kudeh ima magazin za ...?

Where is the ... department?
Къде е отделът за ...?
kudeh eh otdela za ...?

Is there an outdoor market here?
Има ли пазар тук?
ima li pazar took?

When does the market open?
Кога се отваря пазарът?
koga seh otvarya pazara?

I'd like ...
Дайте ми ...
dIteh mi ...

Do you have ...?
Имате ли ...?
imateh li ...?

How much is this?
Колко струва това?
kolko stroova tova?

Where do I pay?
Къде да платя?
kudeh da platya?

Do you take credit cards?
Приемате ли кредитни карти?
pri-emateh li kreditni karti?

I think perhaps you've short-changed me
Струва ми се, че има грешка в рестото
stroova mi seh, cheh ima greshka frestoto

Can I have a receipt?
Бихте ли ми дали касова бележка?
biHteh li mi dali kasova beleshka?

Can I have a bag, please?
Бихте ли ми дали торбичка, моля?
biHteh li mi dali torbichka, molya?

I'm just looking
Само разглеждам
samo razglezhdam

I'll come back later
Ще дойда пак по-късно
shteh doyda pak po kusno

Do you have any more …?
Имате ли още от ...?
imateh li oshteh ot …?

Have you anything cheaper?
Имате ли нещо по-евтино?
imateh li neshto po eftino?

Have you anything larger/smaller?
Имате ли по-голям/по-малък размер?
imateh li po golyam/po maluk razmer?

Can I try it on?
Може ли да го пробвам?
mozheh li da go probvam?

Does it come in other colours?
Имате ли от това в други цветове?
imateh li ottova vdroogi tsvetoveh?

Could you wrap it for me?
Бихте ли го опаковали, моля?
biHteh li go opakovali, molya?

I'd like to change this, please
Бихте ли ми сменили това, мол?
biHteh li mi smenili tova, molya?

I don't have the receipt
Нямам касова бележка
nyamam kasova beleshka

Can I have a refund?
Мога ли да го върна?
moga li da go vurna?

What is the price per kilo?
Каква е цената за килограм?
kakva eh tsenata za kilogram?

Could you write that down?
Бихте ли ми написали това?
biHteh li mi napisali tova?

I'll have a piece of that cheese
Дайте ми парче от това сирене
dIteh mi parcheh ottova sireneh

71

About 250/500 grams
Около двеста и петдесет/петстотин грама
okolo dvesta i pedeset/petstotin grama

A kilo/half a kilo of ..., please
Килограм/половин килограм от ..., моля
kilogram/polovin kilogram ot ..., molya

Can you mend this?
Можете ли да поправите това?
mozheteh li da popraviteh tova?

I'd like this skirt/these trousers dry-cleaned
Искам да оставя тази пола/тези панталони за химическо
    чистене
iskam da ostavya tazi pola/tezi pantaloni za Himichesko chisteneh

When will it/they be ready?
Кога ще бъде готова/бъдат готови?
koga shteh budeh gotova/budat gotovi?

I'd like to make an appointment
Искам да запазя час
iskam da zapazya chas

I want a cut and blow-dry
Подстригване и изсушаване, моля
potstrigvaneh i isooshavaneh, molya

Just a trim, please
Скъсете я съвсем малко, моля
skuseteh ya sufsem malko, molya

A bit more off here, please
Скъсете я още малко тук, моля
skuseteh ya oshteh malko took, molya

Not too much off!
Не я скъсявайте много!
neh ya skusyavIteh mnogo!

72

I don't want any hairspray
Не слагайте лак, моля
neh slagIteh lak, molya

THINGS YOU'LL HEAR

kakvo shteh zhela-eteh?
What would you like?

kazheteh, molya
Can I help you?

suzhalyavam, no tova go svurshiнmeh
I'm sorry, this item is no longer in stock

tova eh fsichko, ko-eto mozhem da vi predlozhim
This is all we have

sheh vi opsloozha slet minoota
I'll be with you in a moment

molya neh pipiteh
Please don't touch

tova li eh fsichko?
Is that all?

shteh zhela-eteh li neshto droogo?
Do you want something else?

imateh li drebni?
Have you got any small change?

eto restoto
Here's the change

kak ya iskateh?
How would you like it?

→

dostatuchno li ya skusih?
Is that short enough?

da vi slozha li lak za kosa?
Would you like hair-spray

da vi slozha li balsam?
Would you like any conditioner?

THINGS YOU'LL SEE

антикварен магазин	*antikvaren magazin*	antiques shop
антикварна книжарница	*antikvarna knizharitsa*	second-hand bookseller
аптека	*apteka*	chemist's
асансьор	*asansyor*	lift
бельо	*belyo*	lingerie, underwear
бижутерия	*bizhooteri-ya*	jeweller's
бирария	*birari-ya*	beer and grills joint, pub
бои и железария	*bo-i i zhelezari-ya*	DIY
бръснарски салон	*brusnarski salon*	barber's shop, men's hairdresser's
вещи под наем	*veshti pod na-em*	items for hire
вино	*vino*	wines
висококачествен	*visokokachestven*	high quality
галантерия	*galanteri-ya*	haberdashery, hosiery
деликатеси	*delikatesi*	delicatessen
домашни потреби	*domashni potrebi*	household goods
евтино	*eftino*	cheap
електроуреди	*elektro-ooredi*	electrical goods
етаж	*etash*	floor

→

74

задруга на майсторите на художествени занаяти	zadrooga na mIstoriteh na hoodozhestveni zana-yati	the Union of Bulgarian Traditional Craftsmen
затворено	zatvoreno	closed
захарни изделия	zaHarni izdeli-ya	confectionery
играчки	igrachki	toys
измиване	izmivaneh	wash
каса	kasa	pay here
кафе	kafeh	coffee shop
килими	kilimi	carpets
кожени изделия	kozheni izdeli-ya	leather goods
книжарница	knizharnitsa	bookshop
конфекция	konfektsi-ya	ready-to-wear clothes
луксозен	looksozen	luxury
магазин бебе	magazin bebeh	babywear
месни изделия	mesni izdeli-ya	sausage meats
месо	meso	meat
млечни продукти	mlechni prodookti	dairy products
мода	moda	fashion
моля вземете кошница	molya vzemeteh koshnitsa	please take a basket
моля не пипайте	molya neh pipIteh	please don't touch
намалени цени	namaleni tseni	reductions
народни занаяти	narodni zana-yati	handicrafts
облекло	obleklo	clothing
обувки	oboofki	footwear
отворено	otvoreno	open
отдел	otdel	department
пазар	pazar	market
партер	parter	ground floor
парфюмерия	parfyoomeri-ya	perfumery
пасмантерия	pasmanteri-ya	haberdashery
платове	platoveh	fabrics

→

плодове и зеленчуци	*plodoveh i zelenchootsi*	fruit and vegetables
поправка на обувки	*poprafka na oboofki*	shoe repairs
подстригване	*podstrigvaneh*	haircut
пресен	*presen*	fresh
приемаме стока	*pri-emameh stoka*	(closed for) taking deliveries
разпродажба	*rasprodazhba*	sale
ревизия	*revizi-ya*	(closed for) stocktaking
РЕП	*rep*	newsagent's
самообслужване	*samo-opsloozhivaneh*	self-service
сирене	*sireneh*	cheese
Съюз на българските художници	*suyoos na bulgarskiteh hoodozhnitsi*	Union of Bulgarian Artists
спиртни напитки	*spirtni napitki*	alcoholic drinks
спортен магазин	*sporten magazin*	sports goods
сутерен	*sooteren*	basement
трикотаж	*trikotash*	knitwear
туристическо бюро	*tooristichesko byooro*	travel agent's
универсален магазин	*ooniversalen magazin*	department store
фризьорски салон	*frizyorski salon*	ladies' hairdresser
химическо чистене	*Himichesko chisteneh*	dry cleaner's
хляб	*Hlyap*	bread
хранителни стоки	*Hranitelni stoki*	grocer's
цветя	*tsvetya*	flowers
цена	*tsena*	price
цигари	*tsigari*	tobacconist's

SPORT

Under communism, nearly all sports facilities in Bulgaria were intended to serve only professional sportsmen and sportswomen. Jogging and sometimes swimming were the only sports which ordinary members of the public could practice.

In the eighties, a few Western-style leisure centres opened in the larger cities, offering aerobics classes and well-equipped gyms, saunas etc. Swimming pools can be found in most larger cities; they are clean but can be overcrowded. Tennis courts are similarly confined to the cities, usually in parks, and are very busy. Both swimming and tennis, as well as mini-golf (but not ordinary golf), are more readily available at coastal resorts. Hiring a bike is also possible at most of the coastal resorts. Facilities for all water sports are available there too, with the possible exception of scuba-diving. A flag warning system operates on most beaches: black means that swimming is temporarily suspended on safety grounds; red is for dangerous conditions and white means all-clear.

Mountaineering and hillwalking are quite popular among Bulgarians and attract an increasing number of visitors to the country.

Skiing is the most popular winter sport in Bulgaria. The two purpose-built ski resorts, Borovets and Pamporovo, have all the usual facilities (ski-tows, chairlifts, equipment hire etc) at reasonable prices. Skiing in Vitosha is also good and has the added attraction of the capital Sofia being only 20 minutes' drive from the hotel area. If package-holiday skiing does not appeal to you, try Bansko and Malyovitsa in the south-west of the country.

Special permits are required for fishing and hunting but 'safari'-type tours can be organized through travel agencies.

USEFUL WORDS AND PHRASES

athletics	атлетика	*atletika*
badminton	бадминтон	*badminton*
ball	топка	*topka*

basketball	баскетбол	*basketbol*
beach	плаж	*plash*
bicycle	велосипед	*velosipet*
bowling	боулинг	*bowlink*
chairlift	открит лифт	*otkrit lift*
fishing	риболов	*ribolof*
fishing rod	въдица	*vuditsa*
football	футбол	*footbol*
football match	футболен мач	*footbolen match*
goggles	очила за плуване	*ochila za ploovaneh*
gymnastics	гимнастика	*gimnastika*
hunting	лов	*lof*
mountaineering	алпинизъм	*alpinizum*
parascending	парашут	*parashoot*
pedal boat	водно колело	*vodno kolelo*
piste	писта	*pista*
racket	ракета	*raketa*
riding	езда	*ezda*
rowing boat	гребна лодка	*grebna lotka*
run *(verb)*	бягам	*byagam*
sailboard	платноходка	*platnoHotka*
sailing	ветроходство	*vetroHotstvo*
skate *(verb)*	карам кънки	*karam kunki*
skates	кънки	*kunki*
ski bindings	ски автомати	*ski aftomati*
ski boots	ски обувки	*ski oboofki*
ski lift	ски лифт	*ski lift*
ski pass	карта за ски лифт	*karta za ski lift*
skis	ски	*ski*
ski tow	ски влек	*ski vlek*
sledge	шейна	*shayna*
snorkel	шнорхел	*shnorHel*
stadium	стадион	*stadi-on*
swim *(verb)*	плувам	*ploovam*
swimming pool	плувен басейн	*plooven basayn*
tennis	тенис	*tenis*
tennis court	тенис корт	*tenis kort*
volleyball	волейбол	*volaybol*

walking	ходене	*Hodeneh*
water-skiing	каране на водни ски	*karaneh na vodni ski*
water-skis	водни ски	*vodni ski*
wet suit	водолазен костюм	*vodolazen kostyoom*
yacht	яхта	*yaHta*

Where can I hire ...?
Къде мога да наема ...?
kadeh moga da na-ema ...?

How do I get to the beach?
Как да отида до плажа?
kak da otida do plazha?

How deep is the water here?
Колко е дълбока водата тук?
kolko eh dulboka vodata took?

Is there an indoor/outdoor pool here?
Тук има ли закрит/открит басейн?
took ima li zakrit/otkrit basayn?

Is it safe to swim here?
Безопасно ли е да се плува тук?
bezopasno li eh da seh ploova took?

Can I fish here?
Тук може ли да се лови риба?
took mozheh li da seh lovi riba?

Do I need a licence?
Необходимо ли е разрешително?
neh-opHodimo li eh razreshitelno?

I would like to hire a sunshade
Искам да наема чадър
iskam da na-ema chadur

How much does it cost per hour/day?
Колко струва на час/на ден?
kolko stroova na chas/na den?

I would like to take water-skiing lessons
Искам да взема уроци по водни ски
iskam da vzema oorotsi povodni ski

Where can I buy skiing equipment?
Къде мога да купя ски оборудване?
kudeh moga da koopya ski oboroodvaneh?

There's something wrong with this binding
Този автомат не работи
tozi aftomat neh raboti

I'd like to try cross-country skiing *(said by a man/woman)*
Бих искал/искала да опитам ски крос
biH iskal/iskala da opitam ski kros

How much is a daily/weekly pass for the skilift?
Колко струва еднодневна/седмична карта за ски лифта?
kolko stroova ednodnevna/sedmichna karta za ski lifta?

Can you recommend a good place to ski?
Бихте ли ми препоръчали подходяща местност за ски?
biHteh li mi preporuchali potHodyashta mesnost za ski?

Where are the nursery slopes?
Къде е пистата за начинаещи?
kudeh eh pistata za nachina-eshti?

THINGS YOU'LL SEE

алея за велосипеди	*aleh-ya za velosipedi*	cycle path
билети	*bileti*	tickets
велосипеди	*velosipedi*	bicycles
влизането забранено	*vlizaneto zabraneno*	restricted area

→

водни спортове	vodni sportoveh	water sports
душове	dooshoveh	showers
закрит плувен басейн	zakrit plooven basayn	indoor swimming pool
играта с топки забранена	igrata stopki zabranena	no ball games
кални бани	kalni bani	mud baths
къпането забранено	kupaneto zabraneno	bathing prohibited
лифт	lift	cable car, chairlift
ловенето на риба забранено	loveneto na riba zabraneno	no fishing
нудистки плаж	noodiski plash	nudist beach
опасно за живота	opasno za zhivota	danger high voltage
опасност от лавини	opasnost ot lavini	danger of avalanche
открит плувен басейн	otkrit plooven basayn	outdoor swimming pool
плаж	plash	beach
плуването забранено	ploovaneto zabreneno	no swimming
скачането забранено	skachaneto zabraneno	no diving
спортен център	sporten tsentur	sports centre
под наем	pod na-em	for hire
платноходки	platnoHotki	sailing boats
пристанищна охрана	pristanishtna oHrana	harbour police
ски влек	ski vlek	ski tow
ски писта	ski pista	ski piste
съблекални жени	sublekalni zheni	women's changing rooms
съблекални мъже	sublekalni muzheh	men's changing rooms
уроци по водни ски	oorotsi po vodni ski	water-skiing lessons
яхт-клуб	yaHt kloop	marina

POST OFFICES AND BANKS

Post offices in Bulgaria can be recognized by a yellow sign. Most post boxes are yellow and so is the sign for telephones. Red letter boxes are supposed to be for express mail but they are used more or less arbitrarily. Sending your mail from the central post office in a town will save you up to a day in delivery time; letters sent by 'express' mail may not be delivered faster and may well be slower than ordinary mail. Anything more than a postcard is worth sending by registered mail **препоръчано писмо** (*preporuchano pismo*) if you want to be sure that it will leave the country intact; this is generally not as expensive as it is in the West. Allow well over a week for a letter or a postcard to arrive at any address in Western Europe. Parcels for abroad have to be taken unwrapped to the post office and wrapped at the counter to allow for examination by a customs official.

Post offices in smaller towns are open from 8.30 am to 5.30 pm and in cities from 8 am to 6 pm Mondays to Saturdays. Post offices in larger cities have a night-duty officer at the telegraph section (for urgent messages only).

The official exchange rate of the major foreign currencies, announced daily by the National Bank, is an advisory one; tourist exchange rates are usually just under this figure. There is no shortage of bureaux de change, **бюро за обмяна** (*byooro za obmyana*), but it will not be necessary or advisable to change more than you will need for the day. Since there is hardly an alternative to paying by cash in Bulgaria, carrying your money around with you seems inevitable (see also HOTELS, page 20).

Changing money with street dealers is still an offence under Bulgarian law and although this law is less strictly enforced since the demise of communism, this activity has lost much of its previous attraction since few of the dealers can match or improve on the official exchange rate, while the possibility of being cheated still remains high. In theory, you are also still required to keep all exchange receipts and be able to produce them on demand when you leave the country.

USEFUL WORDS AND PHRASES

airmail	въздушна поща	*vuzdooshna poshta*
bank	банка	*banka*
banknote	банкнота	*banknota*
cash	пари	*pari*
change *(verb)*	обменям	*obmenyam*
cheque	чек	*chek*
counter	гише	*gisheh*
credit card	кредитна карта	*kreditna karta*
customs form	митническа декларация	*mitnicheska deklaratsi-ya*
delivery	разнасяне	*raznasyaneh*
dollar	долар	*dolar*
envelopes	пликове	*plikoveh*
exchange rate	обменен курс	*obmenen koors*
form	бланка	*blanka*
international money order	международен пощенски превод	*mezhdoonaroden poshtenski prevot*
letter	писмо	*pismo*
letter box	пощенска кутия	*poshtenska kooti-ya*
mail *(noun)*	поща	*poshta*
money order	запис	*zapis*
package/parcel	колет	*kolet*
post *(noun)*	поща	*poshta*
postage rates	пощенска тарифа	*poshtenska tarifa*
postal order	пощенски запис	*poshtenski zapis*
postcard	картичка	*kartichka*
postcode	пощенски код	*poshtenski kot*
poste-restante	до поискване	*do po-iskvaneh*
postman	пощаджия	*poshtaji-ya*
post office	поща	*poshta*
pound sterling	лира стерлинга	*lira stairlinga*
registered letter	препоръчано писмо	*preporuchano pismo*
stamp	марка	*marka*
surface mail	обикновена поща	*obiknovena poshta*
telegram	телеграма	*telegrama*

traveller's cheque	пътнически чек	*putnicheski chek*
writing paper	листи за писма	*listi za pisma*

How much is a letter/postcard to England?
Колко струва писмо/картичка до Англия?
kolko stroova pismo/kartichka do angli-ya?

I'd like four 7-leva stamps
Моля, дайте ми четири марки по седем лева
molya, dlteh mi chetiri marki po sedem leva

I want to register this letter
Искам да изпратя това писмо препоръчано
iskam da ispratya tova pismo preporuchano

I want to send this parcel to England
Искам да изпратя този колет до Англия
iskam da ispratya tozi kolet do angli-ya

Where can I post this?
Къде мога да изпратя това?
kudeh moga da ispratya tova?

Is there any mail for me?
Имате ли поща за мен?
imateh li poshta za men?

I'd like to send a telegram
Искам да изпратя телеграма
iskam da ispratya telegrama

This is to go airmail
Въздушна поща, моля
vuzdooshna poshta, molya

I'd like to change this into leva
Искам да обменя това в левове
iskam da obmenya tova flevoveh

Can I cash these traveller's cheques?
Мога ли да обменя тези пътнически чекове?
moga li da obmenya tezi putnicheski chekoveh?

What is the exchange rate for the pound?
Какъв е обменният курс на лирата?
kakuf eh obmenni-ya koors na lirata?

THINGS YOU'LL SEE

адрес	*adres*	address
банкноти	*banknoti*	banknotes
бърза поща	*burza poshta*	express
бюро	*byooro*	office
бюро за обмяна	*byooro za obmyana*	bureau de change
валута	*valoota*	foreign currency
въздушна поща	*vuzdooshna poshta*	airmail
гише	*gisheh*	teller, counter
гише колети	*gisheh koleti*	parcels counter
директор	*direktor*	(bank) manager
долари	*dolari*	dollars
до поискване	*do po-iskvaneh*	poste-restante
ДСК	*de-seh-ka*	National Savings Bank
запис	*zapis*	money order
затворено	*zatvoreno*	closed
картичка	*kartichka*	postcard
каса	*kasa*	cash desk
касиер	*kasi-er*	cashier
квитанция	*kvitantsi-ya*	receipt
лири стерлинги	*liri stairlingi*	pounds

→

85

марка за страната	marka za stranata	inland postage
марка за чужбина	marka za choozhbina	postage abroad
марки	marki	stamps
монети	moneti	coins
населено място	naseleno myasto	place
отворено	otvoreno	open
пакет	paket	packet
паричен запис	parichen zapis	money order
печатно	pechatno	printed matter
писмо	pismo	letter
подател	podatel	sender
получател	poloochatel	addressee
почивка	pochifka	back in a few minutes
поща	poshta	post office, post, letter box
пощенски код	poshtenski kot	post code
преводи	prevodi	transfers
препоръчани писма	preporuchani pisma	registered mail
работно време	rabotno vremeh	opening hours
сметка	smetka	account
събира се в ...	subira seh v ...	collection times ...
справки	sprafki	information
такса	taxa	charge
тарифа	tarifa	scale of charges
телеграми	telegrami	telegrams
централна поща	tsentralna poshta	central post office
чек	chek	cheque

TELEPHONES

Public phones are easy to come by in all towns. Most of them though are only good for local calls and currently a 20-stotinki piece is necessary for these. In busy places in the towns and around central post offices long-distance payphones may be found, for which you will need 50-stotinki and 1-lev pieces. A similar new type of public phone takes phonecards, which are available from post offices in various denominations. Both coins and cards are difficult to obtain. The quality of international connections is up to Western standards and better than the quality of local and long-distance internal calls.

Making a long-distance or international call is easiest from the telephone sections of post offices. The central ones in most cities stay open until 11 pm, while the one in Sofia never closes and is in fact rather busy at night. You may have to queue for a while until a cabin becomes available. You dial the number yourself and pay afterwards.

At airports and other places frequented by foreigners, Western-style cardphones have been installed and cards can usually be bought nearby for hard currency only.

Phoning abroad from hotels is possible but it is very expensive. To call the UK dial 0044, to call the USA and Canada dial 001, for Australia the code is 0061, for New Zealand 0064 and for Eire 00353. To dial direct, first use the international code and then the STD code minus the initial 0.

The tones you hear on Bulgarian phones are as follows:
Dialling tone : alternate short and long tones;
Ringing : long tones separated by longer pauses;
Engaged : short equal on/off tones.

USEFUL WORDS AND PHRASES

cabin	кабина	*kabina*
call (noun)	телефонен разговор	*telefonen razgovor*
call (verb)	обаждам се по телефона	*obazhdam seh po telefona*
code	код	*kot*
dial (verb)	избирам	*izbiram*
dialling tone	сигнал за избиране	*signal za izbiraneh*
enquiries	справки	*sprafki*
extension	вътрешен номер	*vutreshen nomer*
international call	международен разговор	*mezhdoonaroden razgovor*
number	номер	*nomer*
operator (man)	телефонист	*telefonist*
(woman)	телефонистка	*telefoniska*
payphone	телефонен автомат	*telefonen aftomat*
phonecard	фонокарта	*fonokarta*
receiver	слушалка	*slooshalka*
reverse charge call	разговор "за тяхна сметка"	*razgovor za tyaHna smetka*
telephone	телефон	*telefon*
telephone box	телефонна кабина	*telefonna kabina*
telephone directory	телефонен указател	*telefonen ookazatel*

Where is the nearest phone box?
Къде е най-близката телефонна кабина?
kudeh eh nI-bliskata telefonna kabina?

I would like the directory for Varna
Бихте ли ми дали указателя на Варна?
biHteh li mi dali ookazatelya na Varna?

Can I call abroad from here?
Мога ли да се обадя в чужбина от тук?
moga li da seh obadya fchoozhbina ottook?

How much is a call to London?
Колко струва един разговор до Лондон?
kolko stroova edin razgovor do London?

I would like to reverse the charges
Искам да се обадя "за тяхна сметка"
iskam da seh obadya za tyaнna smetka

I would like a number in the USA *(said by a man/woman)*
Бих искал/искала да се обадя до Съединените Щати
biн iskal/iskala da seh obadya do suh-edineniteh shtati

Hello, this is Anna speaking
Ало, обажда се Анна
alo, obazhda seh Anna

Is that Zhivko?
Живко ли е на телефона?
zhifko li eh na telefona?

Speaking *(said by a man/woman)*
Той/тя е на телефона
toy/tya eh na telefona

I would like to speak to Mr Dimitrov
Мога ли да говоря с г-н Димитров
moga li da govorya zgospodin dimitrof

Extension 283 please
Моля вътрешен двеста осемдесет и три
molya vutreshen dvesta osemdeset itri

Please tell him/her David/Michelle called
Моля, предайте му/и, че Дейвид/Мишел се е обаждал/
    обаждала
*molya, predІteh moo/i, cheh David/Michelle seh eh obazhdal/
    obazhdala*

Ask him/her to call me back please
Моля, предайте му/и да ми се обади
molya, predІteh moo/i da mi seh obadi

TELEPHONES

My number is 22 00 47
Номерът ми е двайсет и две, нула нула, четирисет и седем
nomera mi eh dvIset idveh, noola noola, chetIrset isedem

Do you know where he/she is?
Знаете ли къде е той/тя?
zna-eteh li kudeh eh toy/tya?

When will he/she be back?
Кога ще се върне?
koga shteh seh vurneh?

Could you leave him/her a message ...?
Бихте ли му/и предали ...?
biHteh li moo/i predali ...?

I'll ring back later
Ще позвъня по-късно
shteh pozvunya po-kusno

Sorry, I have the wrong number
Грешка, извинете
greshka, izvineteh

Sorry, you have the wrong number
Имате грешка
imateh greshka

THINGS YOU'LL SEE

автоматично избиране	*aftomatichno izbiraneh*	direct dialling
градски разговор	*gratski razgovor*	local call
код	*kot*	code
международен разговор	*mezhdoonaroden razgovor*	international call

→

междуградски разговор	*mezhdoogratski razgovor*	long-distance call
не работи	*neh raboti*	out of order
повреди	*povredi*	faults service
справки	*sprafki*	enquiries
тарифа	*tarifa*	charges
телефон	*telefon*	telephone
телефонист	*telefonist*	operator
телефонна палата	*telefonna palata*	telephone section
фонокарта	*fonokarta*	phonecard

REPLIES YOU MAY BE GIVEN

skogo iskateh da govoriteh?
Who would you like to speak to?

imateh greshka
You've got the wrong number

koy eh na telefona?
Who's speaking?

koy eh vashi-ya nomer?
What is your number?

suzhalyavam, no nego go/neh-ya ya nyama
Sorry, he/she is not in

toy/tya shteh seh vurneh fshes chasa
He/she will be back at six o'clock

obadeteh seh ootreh, ako obichateh
Please call again tomorrow

shteh mooi predam, cheh steh seh obazhdali
I'll tell him/her you called

EMERGENCIES

Information on local health services can be obtained from tourist information offices. In an emergency, dial 150 for an ambulance, 160 for the fire brigade and 166 for the police. In the event of your car breaking down, phone 146 for help from the Bulgarian Union of Motorists; 163 for breakdown service from the nearest garage; and 162 for General Rescue Services. If you lose your passport, you should notify the British Embassy as well as the police.

Everyone is required to carry an ID card or a passport at all times. Drivers are obliged to have their licences on them and to produce them on demand to the traffic police **KAT** *(kat)*.

Some hotels may keep the passports of foreigners overnight at the reception desk; this is a hangover from the cumbersome procedure for the administration of foreign visitors from communist times and is no cause for alarm.

If you happen to be the injured party in any kind of trouble, you may still be detained by the police (sometimes overnight) until the circumstances are clarified. Patience and a good interpreter will be essential in such cases. If things get difficult, make a point of frequently invoking the name of your Embassy – this should ease matters considerably.

USEFUL WORDS AND PHRASES

accident	злополука	*zlopolooka*
(car)	катастрофа	*katastrofa*
ambulance	линейка	*linayka*
American	Американско	*amerikansko*
Embassy	посолство	*posolstvo*
assault *(verb)*	нападам	*napadam*
breakdown	авария	*avari-ya*
breakdown	аварийна сервизна	*avareena servizna*
recovery	служба	*sloozhba*
break down	повреждa се	*povrezhda seh*

British Embassy	Британско посолство	*britansko posolstvo*
burglar	крадец	*kradets*
burglary	кражба	*krazhba*
casualty department	спешни случаи	*speshni sloocha-i*
crash (*noun*)	сблъскване	*zbluskvaneh*
crash (*verb*)	сблъсквам се	*zbluskvam seh*
fire	пожар	*pozhar*
fire brigade	пожарна команда	*pozharna komanda*
flood (*noun*)	наводнение	*navodneni-eh*
injured	наранен	*naranen*
lose	загубвам	*zagoobvam*
money	пари	*pari*
passport	паспорт	*pasport*
pickpocket	крадец	*kradets*
police	полиция, милиция	*politsi-ya, militsi-ya*
police station	полицейски участък	*politsayski oochastuk*
rob	ограбвам	*ograbvam*
steal	крада	*krada*
theft	кражба	*krazhba*
thief	крадец	*kradets*
tow (*verb*)	тегля	*teglya*

Help!
Помощ!
pomosht!

Look out!
Внимавай!
vnimavI!

Stop!
Спри!
spri!

This is an emergency!
Спешен случай!
speshen sloochI!

EMERGENCIES

Get an ambulance!
Повикайте линейка!
povikIteh linayka!

Please send an ambulance to ...
Моля, изпратете линейка на ...
molya, isprateteh linayka na ...

Please come to ...
Моля, елате на ...
molya, elateh na ...

My address is ...
Адресът ми е ...
adresa mi eh ...

We've had a break-in
В стаята ни са влизали крадци
fstI-ata ni sa vlizali krattsi

There's a fire at ...
Има пожар на ...
ima pozhar na ...

Someone's been injured
Има наранен човек
ima naranen chovek

My passport/car has been stolen
Откраднали са ми паспорта/колата
otkradnali sa mi pasporta/kolata

The registration number is ...
Регистрационният номер е ...
registratsi-onni-ya nomer eh ...

My car's been broken into
Крадци са влезли с взлом в колата ми
krattsi sa vlezli z-vzlom fkolata mi

I've lost my traveller's cheques
Изгубил съм си пътническите чекове
izgoobil sum si putnicheskiteh chekoveh

I want to report a stolen credit card
Искам да съобщя за открадната кредитна карта
iskam da suh-opshtya za otkradnata kreditna karta

It was stolen from my room
Откраднаха го от моята стая
otkradnaHa go ot mo-yata stI-a

I lost it in/at ...
Изгубих го в/на ...
izgoobiH go v/na ...

My luggage has gone missing
Моят багаж го няма
mo-ya bagash go nyama

Has my luggage turned up yet?
Намерен ли е моят багаж?
nameren li eh mo-ya bagash?

I've been mugged
Ограбиха ме на улицата
ograbiHa meh na oolitsata

My son's missing
Синът ми изчезна
sina mi ischezna

He's ... years old
Той е на ... години
toy eh na ... godini

I've locked myself out
Заключих се вън от стаята
zaklyoochiH seh vun ot stI-ata

He's drowning
Той се дави
toy seh davi

She can't swim
Тя не може да плува
tya neh mozheh da ploova

THINGS YOU'LL SEE

болница	*bolnitsa*	hospital
бърза помощ	*burza pomosht*	ambulance
изберете ...	*isbereteh ...*	dial ...
КАТ	*kat*	traffic police
милиция	*militsi-ya*	police, police station
обслужва се 24 часа	*opsloozhva seh 24 chasa*	24-hour service
пожар	*pozhar*	fire
полицейски участък	*politsayski oochastak*	police station
полиция	*politsi-ya*	police, police station
първа помощ	*purva pomosht*	first aid
спасител	*spasitel*	lifeguard
спешни случаи	*speshni sloocha-i*	emergencies
травматология	*travmatologi-ya*	casualty department

THINGS YOU'LL HEAR

koy eh vashi-ya adres?
What's your address?

kadeh steh?
Where are you?

mozheteh li da go opisheteh?
Can you describe it/him?

HEALTH

Under the existing reciprocal agreement British citizens receive free medical treatment in Bulgaria, although they pay for prescriptions. US citizens may have to pay according to the fixed tariffs applicable to foreigners and depending on the complexity of treatment necessary, the circumstances and the disposition of the doctor.

As elsewhere in Europe, pharmacies – **аптека** (*aptęka*) – can give medical advice for minor ailments and first aid if necessary. Practically all medicines that are available can be bought with or without a prescription. Cosmetics, toiletries and accessories are also sold in pharmacies, although it would be unwise to expect the variety of products found in your local chemist's. All towns have one or more pharmacies that are open all night.

For more serious illnesses, you would have to go to the nearest **поликлиника** (*poliklĭnika*) which is a hospital consisting of numerous GPs' and consultants' surgeries – like a very large outpatient department. All **поликлиника** have facilities for performing minor surgery, most of them also have a dispensary on the premises.

In an emergency, an ambulance can be called by phoning 150. The service is free. Bulgarian ambulances do not arrive as fast or as well-equipped as their counterparts in the West but this is no fault of the hard-working staff, rather of the fact that the former communist rulers had a special ambulance service to themselves with vehicles supplied by Mercedes, so they never felt personally compelled to improve the general service.

It will help if you could arrange for an interpreter to accompany you to the doctor but if you cannot, don't panic – most doctors in Bulgaria speak a Western European language. Summon up all your knowledge of German (if you have any), as this is one of the most widely-spoken foreign languages in Bulgaria.

It is advisable to take any medication you need with you and also high-factor sunblock because you may not be able to find what you need, and the latter is unavailable in Bulgarian chemists.

In Sofia, there is a special clinic for foreigners (which is not free of charge) and a chemist's selling Western drugs for hard currency. Ask at the reception desk of any good hotel in the city for directions.

USEFUL WORDS AND PHRASES

accident	злополука	*zlopolooka*
ambulance	линейка	*linayka*
anaemic	анемичен	*anemichen*
appendicitis	апендицит	*apenditsit*
appendix	апендикс	*apendix*
aspirin	аспирин	*aspirin*
asthma	астма	*astma*
backache	болки в гърба	*bolki vgurba*
bandage	превръзка	*prevruska*
bite *(by dog)*	ухапване	*ooHapvaneh*
(by insect)	ужилване	*oozhilvaneh*
bladder	пикочен мехур	*pikochen meHoor*
blister	пришка	*prishka*
blood	кръв	*kruf*
blood donor	кръводарител	*kruvodaritel*
burn *(noun)*	изгаряне	*izgaryaneh*
cancer	рак	*rak*
chemist	аптекар	*aptekar*
chest	гръден кош	*gruden kosh*
chickenpox	шарка, варицела	*sharka, varitsela*
cold *(noun)*	настинка	*nastinka*
concussion	мозъчно сътресение	*mozuchno sutreseni-eh*
constipation	запек	*zapek*
contact lenses	контактни лещи	*kontaktni leshti*
corn	мазол	*mazol*
cough *(noun)*	кашлица	*kashlitsa*
cut *(noun)*	порязване	*poryazvaneh*
dentist	зъболекар	*zubolekar*
diabetes	диабет	*di-abet*
diarrhoea	диария	*di-ari-a*

dizziness	виене на свят	*vi-eneh na svyat*
doctor	лекар	*lekar*
earache	болки в ухото	*bolki fooHoto*
fever	треска	*treska*
filling	пломба	*plomba*
first aid	първа помощ	*purva pomosht*
flu	грип	*grip*
fracture	счупване	*shchoopvaneh*
German measles	дребна шарка, рубеола	*drebna sharka, roobeh-ola*
glasses	очила	*ochila*
haemorrhage	кръвоизлив	*kruvo-izlif*
hayfever	сенна хрема	*senna Hrema*
headache	главоболие	*glavoboli-eh*
heart	сърце	*surtseh*
heart attack	инфаркт	*infarkt*
hospital	болница	*bolnitsa*
ill	болен	*bolen*
indigestion	стомашно разстройство	*stomashno rastroystvo*
injection	инжекция	*inzhektsi-ya*
itch	сърбеж	*surbesh*
kidney	бъбрек	*bubrek*
lump	подутина, бучка	*podootina, boochka*
measles	дребна шарка, морбили	*drebna sharka, morbili*
migraine	мигрена	*migrena*
mumps	заушки	*za-ooshki*
nausea	повдигане	*povdiganeh*
nurse *(female)*	сестра	*sestra*
operation	операция	*operatsi-ya*
optician	оптик	*optik*
pain	болка	*bolka*
penicillin	пеницилин	*penitsilin*
plaster *(sticky)*	лейкопласт	*laykoplast*
plaster of Paris	гипс	*gips*
pneumonia	пневмония	*pnevmoni-ya*
pregnant	бременна	*bremenna*

prescription	рецепта	*retsepta*
rheumatism	ревматизъм	*revmatizum*
scald *(noun)*	изгаряне с вряла течност	*izgaryaneh zvryala technost*
scratch *(noun)*	одраскване	*odraskvaneh*
smallpox	едра шарка, вариола	*edra sharka, vari-ola*
sore throat	възпалено гърло	*vuspaleno gurlo*
splinter *(noun)*	парче	*parcheh*
sprain *(noun)*	изкълчване	*iskulchvaneh*
sting *(noun)*	ужилване	*oozhilvaneh*
stomach	стомах	*stomaH*
temperature	температура	*temperatoora*
tonsils	сливици	*slivitsi*
toothache	зъбобол	*zubobol*
travel sickness	морска болест	*morska bolest*
ulcer	язва	*yazva*
vaccination	ваксинация	*vaksinatsi-ya*
vomit *(verb)*	повръщам	*povrushtam*

I have a pain in ...
Боли ме ...
boli meh ..

I do not feel well
Не се чувствам добре
neh seh choofstvam dobreh

I feel faint *(said by a man/woman)*
Чувствам се отпаднал/отпаднала
choofstvam seh otpadnal/otpadnala

I feel sick
Лошо ми е
losho mi eh

I feel dizzy
Вие ми се свят
vi-eh mi seh svyat

It hurts here
Боли ме тук
boli meh took

It's a sharp pain
Болката е остра
bolkata eh ostra

It's a dull pain
Болката е тъпа
bolkata eh tupa

It hurts all the time
Боли ме непрекъснато
boli meh neprekusnato

It only hurts now and then
Боли ме от време на време
boli meh ot vremeh na vremeh

It hurts when you touch it
Боли ме при допир
boli me pri dopir

It stings
Щипе
shtipeh

It aches
Боли ме
boli meh

I have a temperature
Имам температура
imam temperatoora

I need a prescription for ...
Имам нужда от рецепта за ...
imam noozhda ot retsepta za ...

I normally take ...
Обикновено вземам ...
obiknoveno vzemam ...

I'm allergic to ...
Имам алергия към ...
imam alergi-ya kum ...

Have you got anything for ...?
Имате ли нещо за ...?
imateh li neshto za ...?

Do I need a prescription for ...?
Трябва ли рецепта за ...?
tryabva li retsepta za ...?

I have lost a filling
Падна ми пломбата
padna mi plombata

THINGS YOU'LL SEE

аптека	*apteka*	pharmacy
болница	*bolnitsa*	hospital
бърза помощ	*burza pomosht*	ambulance
дежурнааптека	*dezhoorna-apteka*	duty chemist
зъболекар	*zubolekar*	dentist
кабинет	*kabinet*	surgery
клиника	*klinika*	clinic
лекар	*lekar*	doctor
на празен стомах	*na prazen stomaH*	on an empty stomach
оптик	*optik*	optician
поликлиника	*poliklinika*	hospital outpatients
рентгенология	*rentgenologi-ya*	X-ray department
рецепта	*retsepta*	prescription
спешни случаи	*speshni sloocha-i*	emergencies
уши-нос-гърло	*ooshi-nos-gurlo*	ear, nose and throat department

THINGS YOU'LL HEAR

po ... tabletki na ... chasa
Take ... pills/tablets every ... hours

zvoda
With water

da seh zdufchat
Chew them

edin/dva/tri puti na den
Once/twice/three times a day

samo predi lyaganeh
Only when you go to bed

kakvo vzemateh obiknoveno?
What do you normally take?

tryabva da otideteh na lekar
I think you should see a doctor

suzhalyavam, no tova go nyamameh
I'm sorry, we don't have that

za tova tryabva retsepta
For that you need a prescription

CONVERSION TABLES

DISTANCES

A mile is 1.6km. To convert kilometres to miles, divide the km by 8 and multiply by 5. Convert miles to km by dividing the miles by 5 and multiplying by 8.

miles	0.62	1.24	1.86	2.43	3.11	3.73	4.35	6.21
miles or km	**1**	**2**	**3**	**4**	**5**	**6**	**7**	**10**
km	1.61	3.22	4.83	6.44	8.05	9.66	11.27	16.10

WEIGHTS

The kilogram is equivalent to 2lb 3oz. To convert kg to lbs, divide by 5 and multiply by 11. One ounce is about 28 grams, and eight ounces about 227 grams; 1lb is therefore about 454 grams.

lbs	2.20	4.41	6.61	8.82	11.02	13.23	19.84	22.04
lbs or kg	**1**	**2**	**3**	**4**	**5**	**6**	**9**	**10**
kg	0.45	0.91	1.36	1.81	2.27	2.72	4.08	4.53

TEMPERATURE

To convert Celsius degrees into Fahrenheit, the accurate method is to multiply the °C figure by 1.8 and add 32. Similarly, to convert °F to °C, subtract 32 from the °F figure and divide by 1.8.

°C	-10	0	5	10	20	30	36.9	40	100
°F	14	32	41	50	68	77	98.4	104	212

LIQUIDS

A litre is about 1.75 pints; a gallon is roughly 4.5 litres.

gals	0.22	0.44	1.10	2.20	4.40	6.60	11.00
gals or litres	**1**	**2**	**5**	**10**	**20**	**30**	**50**
litres	4.54	9.10	22.73	45.46	90.92	136.40	227.30

TYRE PRESSURES

lb/sq in	18	20	22	24	26	28	30	33
kg/sq cm	1.3	1.4	1.5	1.7	1.8	2.0	2.1	2.3

MINI-DICTIONARY

a *see page 6*
about: about 16 okolo shesnIset
accelerator pedal za gasta
accident zlopolooka
  (car) katastrofa
accommodation nastanyavaneh
ache bolka
adaptor *(electrical)* adaptor
address adres
adhesive lepilo
after slet
aftershave odekolon za slet
  brusneneh
again otnovo
against protif, sreshtoo
AIDS SPIN
air *(noun)* vuzdooH
air-conditioning klimatichna
  instalatsi-ya
aircraft samolet
air hostess styoo-ardesa
airline avi-okompani-ya
airport letishteh
airport bus aftoboos za letishteto
aisle puteka
alarm clock boodilnik
alcohol alkoHol
all fsichki
  all the streets fsichki oolitsi
  that's all, thanks tova eh
  fsichko, blagodarya
almost pochti
alone sam
already vecheh
always vinagi
am: I am as sum
ambulance linayka
America amerika
American *(man)* amerikanets

(woman) amerikanka
(adj) amerikanski
and i
ankle glezen
another *(different)* drook
  (one more) oshteh edin
  another room drooda stI-a
  another coffee, please oshteh
  edno kafeh, molya
anti-freeze antifris
antique shop antikvaren magazin
antiseptic antiseptichno sretstvo
apartment apartament
aperitif aperitif
appetite apetit
apple yabulka
application form molba
appointment *(business)* sreshta
  (at hairdresser's) chas
apricot kIsi-ya
are: you are vi-eh steh
  (singular, familiar) ti si
  we are ni-eh smeh
  they are teh sa
arm ruka
arrive pristigam
art iskoostvo
art gallery Hoodozhestvena
  galeri-ya
artist Hoodozhnik
as: as soon as possible kolkoto
  seh mozheh po skoro
ashtray pepelnik
asleep: he's asleep toy eh zaspal
aspirin aspirin
at: at the post office fposhtata
  at night prez noshta
  at 3 o'clock ftri chasa
attractive privlekatelen

aunt lelya

Australia afstrali-ya

Australian (man) afstrali-yets
(woman) afstraleeka
(adj) afstraleeski

automatic aftomatichen

away: is it far away? dalecheh li
eh?
go away! ostaveteh meh namira!

awful oozhasen

axe bradva

axle os

baby bebeh

back (not front) otzat
(of body) grup
to come back vrushtam seh

bacon bekon, poosheni gurdi

bad losh

bag torbichka
(handbag) chanta

baggage claim poloochavaneh
na bagash

bagpipes gida

bait struf

bake peka

baker's foorna

balcony balkon

Balkans balkanskiteh strani

ball topka

ballpoint pen Himikalka

banana banan

band (musicians) orkestur

bandage prevruska

bank banka

banknote banknota

bar (for drinks) bar
bar of chocolate parcheh
shokolat

barbecue pecheneh na meso na
otkrito

barber's brusnarski salon

bargain izgodna pokoopka

basement sooteren

basin (sink) mifka

basket koshnitsa

bath (tub) vana
to have a bath vzemam
vana

baths: public baths opshtestvena
banya

bathroom banya, to-aletna

battery bateri-ya

bazaar pazar

beach plash

beans bop

beard brada

beautiful krasif

because zashtoto

bed leglo

bed linen spalno belyo

bedroom spalnya, sti-a

beef govezhdo

beer bira

before ... predi ...

beginner nachina-esht

behind ... zat ...

beige bezhof

below ... doloo ...

belt kolan

beside do

best nidobur

better podobur

between ... mezhdoo ...

bicycle velosipet

big golyam

bikini bikini

bill smetka

bin liner torba za boklook

bird ptitsa

birthday rozhden den
happy birthday! chestit rozhden
den!

birthday card pozdravitelna
kartichka za rozhden den

birthday present podaruk za
rozhden den

biscuit biskv<u>i</u>ta
bite *(noun)* ooH<u>a</u>pvaneh
  (verb) H<u>a</u>pya
bitter gorch<u>i</u>f
black ch<u>e</u>ren
blackberry kup<u>i</u>na
blackcurrant k<u>a</u>sis
Black Sea ch<u>e</u>rno mor<u>e</u>h
blanket odeh-<u>ya</u>lo
bleach *(noun)* bel<u>i</u>na
blind *(cannot see)* slyap
blinds sht<u>o</u>ri
blister pr<u>i</u>shka
blizzard vi-<u>e</u>litsa
blond(e) *(adj)* roos
blood kruf
blouse bl<u>oo</u>za
blue sin
boat k<u>o</u>rap
  (small) l<u>o</u>tka
body t<u>ya</u>lo
boil *(verb)* v<u>a</u>rya
boiler b<u>o</u>yler
bolt *(noun: on door)* rez<u>e</u>h
  (verb) zal<u>o</u>stvam
bone kost
bonnet *(car)* kap<u>a</u>k
book *(noun)* kn<u>i</u>ga
  (verb) zap<u>a</u>zvam
bookshop knizh<u>a</u>rnitsa
boot *(car)* bag<u>a</u>zhnik
  (footwear) bot<u>oo</u>sh
border gr<u>a</u>nitsa
boring sk<u>oo</u>chen
born: I was born in ... rod<u>e</u>n
  sum vuf ...
both idv<u>e</u>teh
  both of us idv<u>a</u>mata
  both ... and ... i ... i ...
bottle boot<u>i</u>lka
bottle-opener otvar<u>a</u>chka za
  boot<u>i</u>lki
bottom d<u>u</u>no
  (part of body) d<u>oo</u>peh

bowl pan<u>i</u>tsa
box koot<u>i</u>-ya
box office k<u>a</u>sa
boy m<u>o</u>mcheh
boyfriend pri-<u>ya</u>tel
bra soot<u>i</u>-en
bracelet gr<u>i</u>vna
brake *(noun)* spir<u>a</u>chka
  (verb) sp<u>i</u>ram
brandy br<u>e</u>ndi
bread Hlyap
breakdown *(car)* povr<u>e</u>da
  I've had a breakdown kol<u>a</u>ta mi
  seh povr<u>e</u>di
breakfast zak<u>oo</u>ska
breathe d<u>i</u>sham
bridge most
  (game) brich
briefcase diplomat<u>i</u>chesko
  k<u>oo</u>farcheh
British brit<u>a</u>nski
brochure brosh<u>oo</u>ra
broken sch<u>oo</u>pen
  broken leg sch<u>oo</u>pen krak
brooch br<u>o</u>shka
brother brat
brown k<u>a</u>fyaf
bruise nat<u>u</u>rtvaneh
brush *(noun)* ch<u>e</u>tka
  (verb: hair) ch<u>e</u>tkam
  (floor) met<u>a</u>
bucket k<u>o</u>fa
building zgr<u>a</u>da
Bulgaria bulg<u>a</u>ri-ya
Bulgarian *(man)* b<u>u</u>lgarin
  (woman) b<u>u</u>lgarka
  (adj) b<u>u</u>lgarski
  the Bulgarians b<u>u</u>lgariteh
bumper br<u>o</u>nya
burglar krad<u>e</u>ts
burn *(noun)* izg<u>a</u>ryaneh
  (verb) g<u>o</u>rya
bus aftob<u>oo</u>s
business b<u>i</u>znes

it's none of your business neh
eh tvo-ya rabota
bus station aftogara
busy *(occupied)* za-eto
(crowded) ozhiven
but no
butcher's mesarnitsa
butter maslo
button kopcheh
buy koopoovam
by: by the window do prozoretsa
by Friday do petuk
by myself sam
written by ... ot ...

cabbage zeleh
cable car zakrit lift
café kafeh-slatkarnitsa
cake torta, pasta
cake shop slatkarnitsa
calculator kalkoolator
call: what's it called? kak seh
kazva?
camcorder videocamera
camera foto-aparat
campsite kumpink
camshaft raspredelitelen val
canal kanal
can *(tin)* konserva
can: can I have ...? biHteh li mi
dali ...?
can you ...? mozheteh li ...?
(familiar) mozhesh li ...?
Canada kanada
Canadian *(man)* kanadets
(woman) kanatka
(adj) kanatski
candle svesht
canoe kanoo
cap *(bottle)* kapachka
(hat) kasket
car leka kola
caravan karavan

carburettor karboorator
card karta
cardigan zhiletka
careful vnimatelen
be careful! vnimavI!
caretaker oorednik
carpet kilim
carriage *(train)* vagon
carrot morkof
carry-cot chanta za noseneh na
bebeh
case *(suitcase)* koofar
cash *(noun)* pari
(verb) osrebryavam
to pay cash plashtam vbroy
cassette kaseta
cassette player kasetofon
castle zamuk
cat kotka
cathedral katedrala
cauliflower karfi-ol
cave peshtera
cemetery grobishteh
central heating parno
centre tsentur
certificate dokooment, svidetelstvo
chair stol
change *(noun: money)* drebni
(verb: money) obmenyam
(clothes) smenyam
cheap eftin
check-in *(desk)* registratsi-ya
nabagazha
cheers! *(toast)* nazdraveh!
cheese sireneh
chemist's apteka
cheque chek
cheque book chekova knishka
cheque card chekova karta
cherry cheresha
chess shaH
chest *(part of body)* gurdi
chewing gum dufka
chicken pileh

child deteh

children detsa

china portselan

chips purzheni kartofi

chocolate shokolat
  box of chocolates kooti-ya shokoladovi bonboni

choir Hor

chop *(food)* purzhola, kotlet
  (verb: cut) seka

Christian name malko imeh

church tsurkva

cigar poora

cigarette tsigara

cinema kino

city grat

city centre gratski tsentur

class klasa

classical music klasicheska moozika

clean *(adj)* chist

clear *(obvious)* yasen
  (water) bistra

clever oomen

clock chasovnik

close *(near)* blizo
  (stuffy) zadooshen
  (verb) zatvaryam

closed zatvoren, zakrit

clothes dreHi

clutch ambreh-ash

coach aftoboos
  (of train) putnicheski vagon

coach station aftogara

coat palto

coathanger zakachalka

cockroach Hlebarka

coffee kafeh

coin moneta

cold *(illness)* nastinka
  (adj) stooden
  I have a cold nastinal sum
  I am cold stoodeno mi eh

collar yaka

collection *(stamps etc)* kolektsi-ya
  (postal) subiraneh na pismata

colour tsvyat

colour film tsveten film

comb *(noun)* greben
  (verb) resha seh

come ela
  I come from ... as sum ot ...
  we came last week ni-eh pristignaHmeh minalata sedmitsa
  come here! ela took!

Communist *(adj)* komoonisticheski

compact disc kompakten disk

compartment koopeh

complicated slozhen

computer kompyootur

concert kontsert

conditioner *(for hair)* balsam

condom prezervatif

congratulations! chestito!

consulate konsoolstvo

contact lenses kontaktni leshti

contraceptive protivozachatuchno sretstvo

cook *(noun)* gotvach
  (verb) gotvya

cooker gotvarska pechka

cooking utensils gotvarski posobi-ya

cool Hladen

cork tapa

corkscrew tirbooshon

corner ugul

corridor koridor

cosmetics kozmetichni sretstva

cost *(verb)* tsena, stoynost
  what does it cost? kolko stroova?

cotton pamook

cotton wool meditsinski pamook

cough *(noun)* kashlitsa
  (verb) kashlyam

country *(state)* durzhava
  (not town) provintsi-ya

cousin *(male)* bratofch**e**t
  (female) bratofch**e**tka
crab rak
cramp sHv**a**shtaneh
crayfish om**a**r
cream smet**a**na
credit card kr**e**ditna k**a**rta
crisps chips
crowded nav**a**litsa
cruise kroo-**i**s
crutches pat**e**ritsi
cry *(weep)* pl**a**cha
  (shout) v**i**kam
cucumber kr**a**stavitsa
cufflinks k**o**pcheta za rukav**e**li
cup ch**a**sha
cupboard shkaf
curtain zav**e**sa
Customs m**i**tnitsa
cut *(noun)* por**ya**zvaneh
  (verb: something) r**e**zha
  to cut oneself por**ya**zvam seh

dad t**a**tko
damp vl**a**zhen
dance *(noun)* tants
  (verb) tants**oo**vam
dangerous op**a**sen
dark t**u**men
  dark blue t**u**mnosin
date d**a**ta
daughter dusht**e**rya
day den
dead m**u**rtuf
deaf gloo**H**
dear *(person)* drak, mil
  (expensive) skup
deckchair sh**e**zlonk
deep dulb**o**k
delayed zak**u**snyal
deliberately nar**o**chno
dentist zubol**e**kar
deodorant dezodor**a**nt

department store ooniv**e**rsalen
  magaz**i**n
departure zamin**a**vaneh
departure lounge z**a**la
  zamin**a**vaneh
develop *(film)* pro-yavy**a**vam
diamond *(jewel)* diam**a**nt
diary dn**e**vnik
dictionary r**e**chnik
die oom**i**ram
different razl**i**chen
  that's different! tov**a** eh n**e**shto
  n**o**vo!
  I'd like a different one m**o**lya,
  d**i**teh mi drook
difficult tr**oo**den
dining room trapez**a**ri-ya
directory *(telephone)* ookaz**a**tel
dirty mr**u**sen
disabled inval**i**t
disposable nappies 'Pampers' ®
distributor *(in car)* raspredel**i**tel
dive *(verb)* gm**oo**rkam seh
divorced *(man)* razv**e**den
  (woman) razv**e**dena
do pr**a**vya
  how do you do? zdrav**a**yteh
  (familiar) zdrav**a**y
doctor l**e**kar
document dokoom**e**nt
dog k**oo**cheh
doll k**oo**kla
dollar d**o**lar
door vrat**a**
double room st**i**-a zdveh legl**a**
doughnut p**o**nichka
down dol**oo**
drawing pin g**a**burcheh
dress r**o**klya
drink *(noun)* nap**i**tka
  (verb) pi-ya
  would you like a drink? **i**skash
  li n**e**shto za pi-**e**neh?
drinking water vod**a** za pi-**e**neh

drive *(verb)* kormoovam
driver shofyor
driving licence shofyorska
  knishka
drunk pi-yan
dry sooH
dry-cleaner's Himichesko
  chisteneh
dummy *(for baby)* biberon
during po vremeh na
dustbin kofa za smet
duster partsal za praH
duty-free bezmiten
duvet yoorgan

each *(every)* fseki
  twenty leva each po dviset
  leva
ear ooHo
  ears ooshi
early rano
earrings obetsi
east istok
easy lesen
eat yam
egg yItseh
either: either of them koyto
  ida-eh
  either … or … ili … ili …
elastic elastichen
elastic band lastik
elbow lakut
electric elektricheski
electricity elektrichestvo
else: something else neshto
  droogo
  someone else nyakoy drook
  somewhere else nyakudeh
  droogadeh
embarrassing smooshtavasht
embassy posolstvo
embroidery broderi-ya
emergency speshen sloochI

emergency brake *(train)*
  vnezapna spirachka
emergency exit pozharen isHot
empty prazen
end krI
engaged *(couple)* zgodeni
  (occupied) za-eto
engine *(motor)* dvigatel
England angli-ya
English *(adj)* angleeski
  (language) angleeski ezik
Englishman anglichanin
Englishwoman anglichanka
enlargement oogolemyavaneh
enough dostatuchno
entertainment razvlecheni-eh
entrance fHot
envelope plik
escalator eskalator
especially osobeno
evening vecher
every fseki
everyone fsichki
everything fsichko
everywhere nafsyakudeh
example primer
  for example naprimer
excellent choodesen
excess baggage svruHbagash
exchange *(verb)* obmenyam
exchange rate obmenen koors
excursion exkoorzi-ya
excuse me! izvineteh!
  (pardon) izvinyavIteh!
exit isHot
expensive skup
extension lead kabelen oodulzhitel
eye oko
  eyes ochi

face litseh
faint *(unclear)* bleden
  (verb) pripadam

fair *(noun)* pana-ir
  it's not fair neh eh chestno
false teeth iskoostveni zubi
family semaystvo
fan *(ventilator)* ventilator
  (football) zapalyanko
  (pop etc) pochitatel
fan belt remuk na oHlazhdaneto
fantastic fantastichen
far daleko
  how far is it to …? kolko eh
  daleko do …?
fare tsena na bilet
farm selsko stopanstvo
farmer zemedelets
fashion moda
fast burs
fat *(person)* debel
  (on meat etc) maznina
father bashta
fax *(noun)* telefax
  (verb) izprashtam telefax
feel *(touch)* choofstvam
  I feel hot goreshto mi eh
  I feel like … iskamishe da …
  I don't feel well neh seh
  choofstvam dobreh
feet kraka
felt-tip pen foolmaster
fence ograda
ferry *(small)* lotka
  (large) feribot
fever treska
fiancé godenik
fiancée godenitsa
field poleh
filling *(in tooth)* plomba
  (in sandwich, cake etc) pulnesh
film film
filter filtur
finger prust
fire ogun
  (blaze) pozhar
fire extinguisher pozharogasitel

fireworks fo-yerverki
first pruf
first aid purva pomosht
first floor purvi etash
fish riba
fishing ribolof
  to go fishing otivam na
  ribolof
fishing rod vuditsa
fishmonger's ribarski magazin
fizzy gaziran
flag znameh
flash *(camera)* svetkavitsa
flat *(level)* plosuk
  (apartment) apartament
flavour fkoos
flea bulHa
flight polet
flippers plavnitsi
floor pot
  (storey) etash
flour brashno
flower tsveteh
fly *(insect)* mooHa
  (verb) letya
fog mugla
folk dancing narodni tantsi
folklore folklor
folk music narodna moozika
food Hrana
food poisoning Hranitelno
  otravyaneh
foot krak
football footbol
for za
  for me za meneh
  what for? za kakvo?
  for a week za edna sedmitsa
foreigner choozhdenets
forest gora
forget zabravyam
fork vilitsa
fortnight dveh sedmitsi
fortress krepost

fountain pen pisalka
fourth chetvurti
free *(not engaged)* svoboden
  (no charge) besplaten
freezer frizer
French frenski
fridge Hladilnik
friend pri-yatel
friendly pri-yatelski
fringe *(hair)* breton
front: in front of ... pret ...
frost mras
fruit plot
fruit juice plodof sok
fry purzha
frying pan tigan
full pulen
  I'm full (up) na-yadoH seh
full board pulen pansi-on
funny smeshen
  (odd) stranen
furniture mebeli

garage garash
garden gradina
garlic chesun
gas-permeable lenses
  gazopronitsa-emi leshti
gate porta
  (at airport) isHot
gay *(homosexual)* Homosexoo-alist
gear *(of car)* skorost
gear lever ruchka za skorostiteh
gel *(for hair)* gel
gents *(toilet)* muzheh
German *(adj)* germanski,
  nemski
get *(fetch, catch)* vzemam
  have you got ...? imash li ...?
  to get the train vzemam vlaka
get back: we get back
  tomorrow ootreh seh
  vrushtameh

to get something back
  vuzvrushtam si
get in vlizam
  (arrive) pristigam
get off *(bus etc)* slizam
get on *(bus etc)* kachvam seh
get out izlizam
get up *(rise)* stavam
gift podaruk
gin jin
girl momicheh
girlfriend pri-yatelka
give davam
glad dovolen
glass *(material)* stuklo
  (for drinking) chasha
glasses ochila
gloss prints glantsirani snimki
gloves rukavitsi
glue lepilo
go otivam
gold zlato
good dobur
  good! dobreh!
goodbye dovizhdaneh
gorge prolom
government pravitelstvo
granddaughter vnoochka
grandfather dyado
grandmother baba
grandparents dyado i baba
grandson vnook
grapes grozdeh
grass treva
Great Britain velikobritani-ya
Greece gurtsi-ya
Greek *(adj)* grutski
  (man) gruk
  (woman) gurkinya
green zelen
grey sif
grill skara, gril
grocer's Hranitelni stoki
ground floor parter

113

groundsheet platnishteh
guarantee *(noun)* garantsi-ya
  (verb) garantiram
guard *(on train)* kondooktor
guide exkoorzovot
guide book putevoditel
guitar kitara
gun *(rifle)* pooshka
  (pistol) pistolet

hair kosa
haircut potstrigvaneh
hairdresser's *(men's)* brusnarski
  salon
  (women's) frizyorski salon
hair dryer seshwar
hair spray lak za kosa
half polovina
  half an hour polovin chas
half board poloopansi-on
ham shoonka
hamburger Hamboorger
hammer chook
hand ruka
handbag damska chanta
handbrake ruchna spirachka
handkerchief nosna kurpa
handle *(of door)* drushka
handsome Hoobaf
hangover maHmoorlook
happy shtastlif
harbour pristanishteh
hard tvurt
  (difficult) trooden
hard lenses tvurdi leshti
hardware shop magazin za
  domashni protrebi izhelezari-ya
hat shapka
have imam
  I don't have ... nyamam ...
  have you got ...? imateh li ...?
hayfever senna Hrema
he toy

head glava
headache glavoboli-eh
headlights faroveh
hear choovam
hearing aid slooHof aparat
heart surtseh
heater pechka, otoplitelen ooret
heating otopleni-eh
heavy tezhuk
heel *(of foot)* peta
  (of shoe) tok
hello zdravay
  (on phone) alo
help *(noun)* pomosht
  (verb) pomagam
her: it's her tya eh
  it's for her za neh-ya eh
  give it to her dI-i go
  her flat nayni-ya apartament
  her book naynata kniga
  her name naynoto imeh
  her shoes nayniteh oboofki
  it's hers nayno eh
hi! zdrasti!
high visok
hill Hulm
him: it's him toy eh
  it's for him za nego eh
  give it to him dI moo go
hire: for hire pod na-em
his: his flat negovi-ya
  apartament
  his book negovata kniga
  his name negovoto imeh
  his shoes negoviteh oboofki
  it's his negovo eh
history istori-ya
hitchhike dvizha seh na aftostop
hobby Hobi
holiday praznik
home: at home fkushti
honest chesten
honey met
honeymoon meden mesets

horn *(of car)* klakson
  (of animal) rok
horrible oozhasen
hospital bolnitsa
hot-water bottle grayka
hour chas
house kushta
how? kak?
hungry: I'm hungry gladen sum
hurry: I'm in a hurry burzam
husband suprook

I as
ice let
ice cream sladolet
ice skates kunki za let
ice skating: to go ice skating
  karam kunki na let
icon ikon
if ako
ignition zapalvaneh
ill bolen
immediately vednaga
impossible nevuzmozhen
in v
  in English na angleeski
  in the hotel fHotela
  in Sofia fsofia
indicator pokazatel
indigestion stomashno
  rastroystvo
infection infektsi-ya
information informatsi-ya
injection inzhektsi-ya
injury naranyavaneh
ink mastilo
inn Han
inner tube vutreshna gooma
insect nasekomo
insect repellent sretstvo protif
  nasekomi
insomnia bessuni-eh
instant coffee neskafeh

insurance zastraHofka
interesting interesen
interpret prevezhdam oostno
interpreter prevodach
invitation pokana
Ireland irlandi-ya
Irish irlantski
Irishman irlandets
Irishwoman irlantka
iron *(material)* zhelyazo
  (for clothes) yooti-ya
  (verb) gladya
is: he/she/it is ... toy/tya/to
  eh ...
island ostrof
it to
its negof

jacket yakeh
  (of suit) sako
jam konfityoor, slatko
jazz jas
jeans jinsi, dunki
jellyfish medooza
jeweller's bizhooteri-ya
job rabota, zanimani-eh
jog *(verb)* ticham za zdraveh
  to go for a jog izlizam da ticham
joke shega
journey putoovaneh
jumper poolover
just *(only)* samo
  I've just one left ostanal mi eh
  samo edin
  it's just arrived tokoo shto
  pristigna

kettle chinik
key klyooch
kidney bubrek
kilo kilo, kilogram
kilometre kilometur

kitchen kooHnya
knee kolyano
knife nosh
knit pleta
knitwear trikotash
know: I don't know neh zna-ya

label etiket
lace dantela
laces *(of shoe)* vruski
ladies *(toilet)* zheni
lady dama, zhena
lake ezero
lamb *(meat)* agneshko
lamp lampa
lampshade abazhoor
land *(noun)* zemya
  (verb) katsam
language ezik
large golyam
last *(final)* posleden
  last week minalata sedmitsa
  at last! ni posleh!
late zakusnyal
  the bus is late aftoboosa ima
  zakusneni-eh
later po-kusno
laugh *(noun)* smyaH
laundry *(place)* peralnya
  (dirty clothes) praneh
laxative rasslabitelno sretstvo
lazy murzelif
leaf list
leaflet broshoora
learn oocha
leather kozha
left *(not right)* lyaf
  there's nothing left nishto neh
  eh ostanalo
left-luggage locker kabini za
  bagash
left-luggage office garderop
leg krak

lemon limon
lemonade limonada
length dulzhina
lens leshta
  (of camera) obektif
less po-malko
lesson oorok
letter pismo
  (of alphabet) bookva
letterbox poshtenska kooti-ya
lettuce maroolya
library bibli-oteka
licence razreshitelno
life zhivot
lift *(in building)* asansyor
  could you give me a lift? shteh
  meh otkarash li skolata?
light *(noun)* svetni lampata
  (adj: not heavy) lek
  (not dark) svetul
light bulb krooshka
light meter svetlomer
lighter zapalka
lighter fuel gorivo za
  raspalvaneh
like: I like you Haresvam teh
  I like swimming obicham da
  ploovam
  it's like ... kato ... eh
  like this one kato tozi
lip salve meHlem za oosni
lipstick chervilo
liqueur likyor
list spisuk
litre litur
litter booklook
little *(small)* maluk
  it's a little big malko eh golyam
  just a little sufsem malko
liver cheren drop
lobster omar
lollipop karamel na klechka
long duluk
lorry kami-on

lost property office byooro za
    izgoobeni veshti
lot: a lot mnogo
loud silen
    (colour) yaruk
lounge fwa-eh
love *(noun)* lyoobof, obich
    (verb) obicham
low nisuk
    (voice) tiH
luck kusmet
    good luck! nadobur chas!
luggage bagash
luggage rack bagazhnik
lunch obyat

mad loot
magazine spisani-eh
mail poshta
make pravya
make-up grim
man mush
manager *(in hotel etc)* oopravitel
many: not many neh mnogo
map karta
    a map of Sofia karta na sofia
marble mramor
margarine margarin
market pazar
marmalade marmalat
married *(man)* zhenen
    (woman) omuzhena
mascara spirala
mass *(church)* sloozhba
mast machta
match *(light)* klechka kibrit
    (sport) mach
material *(cloth)* plat
matter: it doesn't matter
    nyama znacheni-eh
mattress dyooshek
maybe mozheh bi
me: it's me as sum

it's for me za meneh eh
give it to me dI mi go
meal yadeneh
mean: what does this mean?
    kakvo znachi tova?
meat meso
mechanic meHanik
medicine lekarstvo
medium *(steak)* sredno
    opechena
medium-sized sreden rust
meeting sreshta
melon pupesh
menu menyoo
message su-opshteni-eh
midday obet
middle: in the middle fsredata
midnight poloonosht
milk mlyako
mine: it's mine mo-eh eh
mineral water mineralna voda
minute minoota
mirror ogledalo
Miss gospozhitsa
mistake greshka
monastery manastir
money pari
month mesets
monument pametnik
moon loona
moped motopet
more oshteh
morning sootrin
    in the morning sootrinta
mosaic mozIka
mosque jami-ya
mosquito komar
mother mIka
motorbike mototsiklet
motorboat kater, motorna lotka
motorway aftomagistrala
mountain planina
mountain pass planinski proHot
mouse mishka

mousse *(for hair)* moos za kosa
moustache moostatsi
mouth oosta
move: please move your car
  biHteh li si premestili kolata?
  don't move! neh murdi!
Mr gospodin
Mrs gospozha
mug chasha zdrushka
mum mama
mural stenopis
museum moozay
mushroom guba
music moozika
musical instrument moozikalen
  instrooment
musician moozikant
mussels midi
must: I must ... tryabva da ...
mustard gorchitsa
my: my flat mo-ya apartament
  my handbag mo-yata chanta
  my name mo-eto imeh
  my keys mo-iteh klyoochoveh

nail *(metal)* gvozday
  (finger) nokut
nail clippers rezachka za nokti
nail file pila za nokti
nail polish lak za nokti
name imeh
  what's your name? kak seh
  kazvash?
nappy pelenka
narrow tesen
near ... blizo do ...
necessary ne-opHodim
neck vrat
necklace gerdan
need *(verb)* noozhda-ya seh
  I need ... imam noozhda ot ...
  there's no need nyama
  noozhda

needle igla
negative *(noun)* negatif
neither: neither of them nito
  edin ot tyaH
  neither ... nor ... nito ...
  nito ...
nephew plemennik
never nikoga
new nof
news novini
newsagent rep
newspaper vesnik
New Zealand nova zelandi-ya
New Zealander *(man)*
  novozelandets
  (woman) novozelantka
next sledvasht
  next week sledvashtata
  sedmitsa
  what next? kakvo oshteh?
nice *(attractive)* Hoobaf
  (pleasant) pri-yaten
  (to eat) fkoosen
niece plemennitsa
night nosht
nightclub noshten bar
nightdress vecherno obleklo
night porter noshten porti-er
no *(response)* neh
  no ... nikakuf ...
  I have no money nyamam pari
noisy shoomen
north sever
Northern Ireland severna
  irlandi-ya
nose nos
not neh
  he's not ... toy neh eh ...
notebook belezhnik
nothing nishto
novel roman
now sega
nowhere nikudeh
number nomer

number plate registratsi-<u>o</u>nen n<u>o</u>mer

nursery slope p<u>i</u>sta za nachina-<u>e</u>shti

nut *(fruit)* <u>ya</u>tka
  (for bolt) g<u>i</u>ka

occasionally pon<u>ya</u>koga

of na

office kant<u>o</u>ra, kantsel<u>a</u>ri-ya

often ch<u>e</u>sto

oil masl<u>o</u>

ointment meHl<u>e</u>m

OK d<u>o</u>br<u>e</u>h

old star
  how old are you? na k<u>o</u>lko si g<u>o</u>dini?

olive masl<u>i</u>na

omelette oml<u>e</u>t

on ... vurH<u>oo</u> ...

one ed<u>i</u>n

onion look

only s<u>a</u>mo

open *(verb)* otv<u>a</u>ryam
  (adj) otv<u>o</u>ren

operation oper<u>a</u>tsi-ya

operator *(man)* telefon<u>i</u>st
  (woman) telefon<u>i</u>stka

opposite: opposite the hotel sresht<u>oo</u> Hot<u>e</u>la

optician opt<u>i</u>k

or il<u>i</u>

orange *(colour)* or<u>a</u>nzhef
  (fruit) portok<u>a</u>l

orange juice portok<u>a</u>lof sok

orchestra ork<u>e</u>stur

ordinary obiknov<u>e</u>n

Orthodox pravosl<u>a</u>ven

other: the other ... dr<u>oo</u>gi-ya ...

our nash
  it's ours n<u>a</u>sheh eh

out vun
  he's out n<u>e</u>go go n<u>ya</u>ma

outside nav<u>u</u>n

oven f<u>oo</u>rna

over *(more than)* nat
  (finished) kr<u>I</u>
  it's over the road ot dr<u>oo</u>gata stran<u>a</u> na p<u>u</u>tya eh
  over there ay tam

overtake isprev<u>a</u>rvam

pack of cards kol<u>o</u>da k<u>a</u>rti

package *(parcel)* pak<u>e</u>t

packet: a packet of ... pak<u>e</u>t ...

padlock katin<u>a</u>r

page str<u>a</u>nitsa

pain b<u>o</u>lka

painkiller analg<u>i</u>n ®

paint *(noun)* bo-<u>ya</u>

pair chift

palace dvor<u>e</u>ts

pale blet

pancakes palach<u>i</u>nki

paper Hart<u>i</u>-ya
  (newspaper) v<u>e</u>snik

paraffin keros<u>i</u>n

parcel kol<u>e</u>t

pardon? m<u>o</u>lya?

parents rod<u>i</u>teli

park *(noun)* park
  (verb) park<u>i</u>ram

parting *(in hair)* put

party *(celebration)* g<u>o</u>sti, sub<u>i</u>raneh
  (group) komp<u>a</u>ni-ya
  (political) part<u>i</u>-ya

passenger p<u>u</u>tnik

passport pasp<u>o</u>rt

pasta makar<u>o</u>ni

path put<u>e</u>ka

pavement p<u>u</u>tna nast<u>i</u>lka

pay pl<u>a</u>shtam

peach pr<u>a</u>skova

peanuts fust<u>u</u>tsi

pear kr<u>oo</u>sha

pearl perla
peas graH
pedestrian pesheHodets
peg (for clothes) shtipka
  (for tent) kolcheh
pen pisalka
pencil molif
pencil sharpener ostrilka
penknife jobno noshcheh
people Hora
pepper piper
per: per night na nosht
perfect ideh-alen
perfume parfyoom
perhaps mozheh bi
perm kudreneh
petrol benzin
petrol station benzinostantsi-ya
photograph (noun) snimka
  (verb) snimam, fotografiram
photographer fotograf
phrase book razgovornik
piano pi-ano
pickpocket kradets
picnic piknik
piece parcheh
pillow vuzglavnitsa
pin topleeka
pineapple ananas
pink rozof
pipe (for smoking) loola
  (for water) truba
Pirin Mountains pirin
  planina
piston bootalo
pizza pitsa
place myasto
  at your place oovas
plant rasteni-eh
plaster (for cut) laykoplast
plastic (adj) plasmasof
plastic bag nilonof plik
plate chini-ya
platform peron

play (theatre) pi-esa
  (verb) igra-ya
please molya
plug (electrical) shtepsel
  (for sink) zapooshalka
pocket jop
poison otrova
police politsi-ya
policeman politsI
police station politsayski
  oochastuk
poor beden
  (bad) losh
pop music pop moozika, estradna
  moozika
pork svinsko meso
port (harbour) pristanishteh
  (drink) port
porter (hotel) porti-er
possible vuzmozhen
post (noun) poshta
  (verb) prashtam po poshtata
post box poshtenska kooti-ya
postcard poshtenska kartichka
poster afish, plakat
postman poshtaji-ya
post office poshta
potato kartof
poultry (meat) pileshko meso
pound (money) lira sterlinga
  (weight) foont
powder (medicine) praH
  (for face) poodra
pram detska kolichka
prawn edra skarida
prefer pretpochitam
prescription retsepta
pretty (beautiful) Hoobaf
  (quite) dosta
  pretty good dosta
priest dosta dobur
private chasten
problem problem
public opshtestven

pull durpam
puncture spookvaneh na gooma
purple moraf
purse portmoneh
push bootam
pushchair detska sportna
  kolichka
put slagam
pyjamas pizhama

quality kachestvo
quarter chetvurt
quay kay
question vupros
queue *(noun)* opashka
  (verb) redya se na opashka
quick burs
quiet tiH
quite *(fairly)* dosta
  (fully) sufsem

radiator radi-ator
radio radi-o
radish repichka
railway zhelezoputna lini-ya
rain dusht
raincoat duzhdobran
raisins stafidi
raspberry malina
rare *(uncommon)* ryaduk
  (steak) nedopechen
rat pluH
razor blades noshcheta za
  brusneneh
read cheta
ready gotof
rear lights stopoveh
receipt kvitantsi-ya
receptionist *(man)* administrator
  (woman) administratorka
record *(music)* gramofonna
  plocha

  (sporting etc) rekort
record player gramofon
record shop magazin za plochi
red cherven
  (hair) rizha
refreshments zakooski
registered letter preporuchano
  pismo
relative rodnina
relax otpooskam seh
religion religi-ya
remember pomnya
  I remember spomnyam si
  I don't remember neh si
  spomnyam
rent *(verb)* na-emam
reservation rezervatsi-ya
rest *(noun: remainder)* ostatuk
  (verb: relax) pochivam si
restaurant restorant
return *(come back)* vrushtam seh
  (give back) vrushtam
return ticket bilet za otivaneh i
  vrushtaneh
rice oris
rich bogat
right *(correct)* pravilen
  (not left) desen
Rila Mountains rila planina
ring *(on finger)* prusten
  (verb: call) zvunya
ripe zryal
river reka
road put
rock *(stone)* kamuk
  (music) rok
roll *(bread)* Hlepcheh
Romania roomuni-a
Romanian roomunski
  (man) roomunets
  (woman) roomunka
roof pokrif
room stI-a
  (space) myasto

rope vuzheh
rose roza
round *(circular)* krugul
  it's my round moy ret eh
rowing boat grebna lotka
rubber *(material)* gooma
  (eraser) goomichka
rubbish smet, boklook
ruby *(stone)* roobin
rucksack ranitsa
rug *(mat)* kilimcheh
  (blanket) odeh-yalo
ruins razvalini
ruler *(for drawing)* lini-ya
rum rom
run *(verb)* byagam

sad tuzhen
safe *(not in danger)* bezopasen
safety pin bezopasna igla
sailing boat platnoHotka
salad salata
salami salam 'zakooska' ®
sale *(at reduced prices)*
  rasprodazhba
salmon syomga
salt sol
same: the same dress sushtata
  roklya
  same again, please oshteh ot
  sushtoto, molya
sand pyasuk
sandals sandali
sandwich sandvich
sanitary towels damski prevruski
sauce sos
saucepan tenjera
sauna sa-oona
sausage salam
say kazvam
  what did you say? kakvo kaza?
  how do you say ...? kak da
  kazha ...?

scarf shalcheh
  (head) kurpa za glava
school oochilishteh
scissors nozhitsi
Scotland shotlandi-ya
Scotsman shotlandets
Scotswoman shotlantka
Scottish shotlantski
screw vint
screwdriver otverka
sea moreh
seat myasto
seat belt pretpazen kolan
second *(of time)* sekoonda
  (in series) ftori
see vizhdam
  I can't see neh moga da vidya
  I see razbiram
sell prodavam
sellotape ® lepenka, skoch
send isprashtam
separate otdelen
separated otdelen
serious seri-ozen
serviette salfetka
several nyakolko
sew shi-ya
shampoo shampwan
shave *(noun)* brusneneh
  to have a shave brusna seh
shaving foam pyana za
  brusneneh
shawl shal
she tya
sheet charshaf
shell cheroopka
sherry sheri
ship korap
shirt riza
shoe laces vruski za oboofki
shoe polish bo-ya za oboofki
shoes oboofki
shoe shop magazin za oboofki
shop magazin

shopping pazaroovaneh
  to go shopping pazaroovam
short *(sleeve etc)* kus
  (person) nisuk
shorts shorti
shoulder ramo
shower *(bath)* doosh
  (rain) lek dusht
shrimp skarida
shutter *(camera)* zatvor
  (window) kepenk
sick *(ill)* bolen
  I feel sick povrushta mi seh
  to be sick *(vomit)* povrushtam
side *(edge)* strana
sidelights stranichni svetlini
sights: the sights of ...
  zabelezhitel-nostiteh na ...
silk koprina
silver *(colour)* srebrist
  (metal) srebro
simple prost
sing peh-ya
single *(one)* edin
  (unmarried: man) nezhenen
  (woman) ne-omuzhena
single room edinichna sti-a
sister sestra
skate kunka
skates kunki
ski *(verb)* karam ski
ski binding ski aftomat
ski boots ski oboofki
skid *(verb)* booksoovam
skiing: to go skiing otivam da
  karam ski
ski lift ski lift
skin cleanser losi-on
ski resort ski koorort
skirt riza
skis ski
ski sticks shteki
sky nebeh
sledge shayna

sleep *(noun)* sun
  (verb) spya
  to go to sleep zaspivam
sleeper spalen vagon
sleeping bag spalen chooval
sleeping pill sunotvorno
  Hapcheh
slippers cheHli
slow baven
small maluk
smell *(noun)* mirizma
  (verb) mirisha
smile *(noun)* oosmifka
  (verb) oosmiHvam seh
smoke *(noun)* pooshek
  (verb) poosha
snack zakooska
snorkel shnorHel
snow snyak
so: so good tolkova Hoobavo
  not so much neh tolkova mnogo
soaking solution *(for contact
  lenses)* rastvor za kontaktni leshti
soap sapoon
socks chorapi
soda water gazirana voda, soda
soft lenses meki leshti
somebody nyakoy
somehow nyakaksi
something neshto
sometimes ponyakoga
somewhere nyakudeh
son sin
song pesen
sorry! *(apology)* izvinyavIteh!
  I'm sorry izvinyavIteh
  sorry? *(pardon)* molya?
soup soopa
south yook
souvenir soovenir
spade lopata
spanner ga-echen klyooch
spares rezervni chasti
spark(ing) plug svesht

speak govorya
  do you speak ...? govoriteh li ...?
  I don't speak ... neh govorya ...
speed skorost
speed limit ogranicheni-eh na skorosta
speedometer spidometur
spider pl-ak
spinach spanak
spoon luzhitsa
sports centre sporten tsentur
spring *(mechanical)* proozhina
  (season) prolet
square *(noun: in town)* ploshtat
  (adj: in shape) kvadrat
stadium stadi-on
staircase stulbishteh
stairs stulbi
stamp marka
stapler telbot
star zvezda
  (film) filmova zvezda
start *(noun: beginning)* nachalo
  (verb) trugvam
  (work etc) zapochvam
station gara
statue statoo-ya
steak purzhola
steal krada
  it's been stolen otkradnato eh
steamer *(boat)* paraHot
steering wheel kormilo
sting *(noun)* zhilo
  (verb) zhilya
  it stings shtipeh
stockings damski chorapi
stomach stomaH
stomach ache bolki fstomaHa
stop *(noun: for bus)* spirka
  (verb) spiram
  stop! spreteh!
storm boorya

strawberry yagoda
stream *(small river)* roochay
street oolitsa
string *(cord)* vruf
  (of guitar etc) stroona
strong *(person, drink)* silen
  (material) zdraf
student student
stupid tup
suburbs predgradi-ya
sugar zaHar
suit *(noun)* kostyoom
  it suits you otiva ti
suitcase koofar
sun sluntseh
sunbathe peka seh na sluntseh
sunburn slunchevo izgaryaneh
sunglasses ochila za sluntseh
sunny: it's sunny vremeto eh slunchevo
sunshade chadur
suntan: to get a suntan pochernyavam ot sluntseto
suntan lotion plazhno mlyako
suntanned pochernyal
supermarket soopermarket
supper vecherya
supplement dobafka
sure sigooren
  are you sure? sigooren li si?
surname familno imeh
sweat *(noun)* pot
  (verb) potya seh
sweatshirt antsook
sweet *(not sour)* sladuk
  (candy) bonbon
swim *(verb)* ploovam
swimming costume banski kostyoom
swimming pool plooven basayn
swimming trunks ploofki
switch klyooch
synagogue sinagoga

table masa
tablet tabletka
take vzemam
take-away *(food)* Hrana zafkushti
take-off izlitaneh
talcum powder talk
talk *(noun)* razgovor
  (verb) govorya
tall visok
tampons tamponi
tangerine mandarina
tap kran
tapestry goblen
tea chI
teacher oochitel
tea towel kurpa za sudoveh
telegram telegrama
telephone *(noun)* telefon
  (verb) obazhdam seh
telephone box telefonna kabina
telephone call telefonno
  obazhdaneh
television televizi-ya
temperature temperatoora
tent palatka
tent peg kolcheh
tent pole to-yashka za palatka
than otkolkoto
thank blagodarya
  thank you/thanks blagodarya
that *(that one)* onova
  that man onzi chovek
  that woman onazi zhena
  that seat onova myasto
  what's that? kakvo eh onova?
  I think that ... mislya, cheh ...
the -ut/-yat *(m)*, -ta *(f)*, -to *(n)*;
  (plural) -te *(m/f)* -ta *(n); see
  pages 5-6*
their: their flat teHni-ya
  apartament
  their room tyaHnata sti-a
  their school tyaHnoto
  oochilishteh

their books teHniteh knigi
it's theirs tyaHno eh
them: it's them teh sa
  it's for them za tyaH eh
  give it to them dI-im go
then togava
  (after) slet tova
there tam
  there is/are ... ima ...
  is/are there ...? ima li ...?
Thermos flask ® termos
these tezi
they teh
thick debel
thin tunuk
think mislya
  I think so taka mislya
  I'll think about it shteh si
  pomislya
third treti
thirsty: I'm thirsty zhaden sum
this *(this one)* tova
  this man tozi mush
  this woman tazi zhena
  this seat tova myasto
  what's this? kakvo eh tova?
  this is Mr ... tova eh gospodin ...
those onezi
throat gurlo
throat pastilles bonboni za gurlo
through pres
thunderstorm grumotevichna
  boorya
ticket bilet
ticket office kasa za bileti
tide prilif
tie *(noun)* vratovruska
  (verb) vruzvam
tight stegnat
tights chorapogashti
time vremeh
  what's the time? kolko eh chasa?
timetable *(train, bus)* raspisani-eh
tin konserva

tin-opener otvar<u>a</u>chka za kons<u>e</u>rvi
tip *(money)* baksh<u>i</u>sh
  (end) kr<u>i</u>cheh
tired izmor<u>e</u>n
tissues kn<u>i</u>zhna k<u>u</u>rpichka
to: to England do <u>a</u>ngli-ya
  to the station do g<u>a</u>rata
  to the doctor na l<u>e</u>kar
toast prep<u>e</u>chen Hlyap
tobacco tyoot<u>yoo</u>n
toboggan sp<u>o</u>rtna shayn<u>a</u>
today dnes
together z<u>a</u>-edno
toilet to-al<u>e</u>tna
toilet paper to-al<u>e</u>tna Hart<u>i</u>-ya
tomato dom<u>a</u>t
tomato juice dom<u>a</u>ten sok
tomorrow <u>oo</u>treh
tongue ez<u>i</u>k
tonic t<u>o</u>nik
tonight dov<u>e</u>chera
too *(also)* s<u>u</u>shto
  (excessively) prekal<u>e</u>no
tooth zup
toothache zubob<u>o</u>l
toothbrush ch<u>e</u>tka za z<u>u</u>bi
toothpaste p<u>a</u>sta za z<u>u</u>bi
torch fen<u>e</u>rcheh
tour obik<u>o</u>lka
tourist toor<u>i</u>st
tourist office toorist<u>i</u>chesko
  byoor<u>o</u>
towel Havl<u>i</u>-ya
tower k<u>oo</u>la
town grat
town hall km<u>e</u>tstvo
toy igr<u>a</u>chka
toy shop magaz<u>i</u>n za igr<u>a</u>chki
track suit <u>a</u>ntsook ikl<u>i</u>n
tradition trad<u>i</u>tsi-ya
traffic dvizh<u>e</u>ni-eh
traffic lights svetof<u>a</u>r
trailer remark<u>e</u>h

train vlak
trainers marat<u>o</u>nki
translate prev<u>e</u>zhdam p<u>i</u>smeno
translator prevod<u>a</u>ch
travel agency byoor<u>o</u> za toor<u>i</u>zum
traveller's cheque p<u>u</u>tnicheski chek
tray podn<u>o</u>s
tree durv<u>o</u>
trousers pantal<u>o</u>ni
true v<u>e</u>ren
try op<u>i</u>tvam
tunnel toon<u>e</u>l
Turk *(man)* t<u>oo</u>rchin
  (woman) toork<u>i</u>nya
Turkey t<u>oo</u>rtsi-ya
Turkish *(adj)* t<u>oo</u>rski
tweezers pints<u>e</u>ti
typewriter p<u>i</u>sheshta mash<u>i</u>na
tyre aftomob<u>i</u>lna g<u>oo</u>ma

umbrella chad<u>u</u>r
uncle *(father's brother)* ch<u>i</u>cho
  (mother's brother) v<u>oo</u>-icho
under ... pot ...
underpants d<u>o</u>lni gasht<u>e</u>ta
underskirt f<u>oo</u>sta
understand razb<u>i</u>ram
  I don't understand neh razb<u>i</u>ram
underwear bely<u>o</u>
university oonivers<u>i</u>tet
unleaded bezol<u>o</u>ven
unmarried *(man)* nezh<u>e</u>nen
  (woman) ne-om<u>u</u>zhena
until dok<u>a</u>to
unusual ne-obikn<u>o</u>ven
up nag<u>o</u>reh
  up there tam g<u>o</u>reh
urgent sp<u>e</u>shen
us: it's us n<u>i</u>-eh smeh
  it's for us zan<u>a</u>s eh
  give it to us d<u>i</u>teh ni go

use *(noun)* oopotr**e**ba, isp**o**lzvaneh
    (verb) oopotreb**ya**vam, isp**o**lzvam
  it's no use bespol**e**zno eh
useful pol**e**zen
usual obiknov**e**n
usually obiknov**e**no

vacancy *(room)* svob**o**dna st**i**-a
vacuum cleaner praHosmook**a**chka
valley dol**i**na
valve kl**a**pa
vanilla van**i**li-ya
vase v**a**za
veal tel**e**shko
vegetable zelench**oo**k
vegetarian *(noun)* vegetari-**a**nets
    (adj) vegetari-**a**nski
vehicle prev**o**zno sr**e**tstvo
very (much) mn**o**go
vest p**o**tnik
video *(tape)* v**i**deokaseta
    (film) v**i**deofilm
video recorder v**i**deo
view **i**zglet
viewfinder viz**yo**r
villa v**i**la
village s**e**lo
vinegar ots**e**t
visa v**i**za
visit *(noun: to person)* gost**oo**vaneh
    (to place) posesht**e**ni-eh
    (verb: person) gost**oo**vam na
    (place) poshesht**a**vam
visitor *(to museum etc)* poset**i**tel
    (guest) gost
vitamin tablet vitam**i**n
vodka v**o**tka
voice glas

wait ch**a**kam
  wait! chak**i**!
waiter servit**yo**r
  waiter! izvin**e**teh!
waiting room chak**a**lnya
waitress servit**yo**rka
  waitress! izvin**e**teh!
Wales Wels
walk *(noun: stroll)* rasH**o**tka
    (verb) H**o**dya
  to go for a walk ot**i**vam na rasH**o**tka
walkman ® w**o**kman
wall sten**a**
wallet portf**a**yl
war voyn**a**
wardrobe garder**o**p
warm t**o**pul
was: I was as byaH
  he was toy b**e**sheh
  she was tya b**e**sheh
  it was to b**e**sheh
washing powder praH za pran**e**h
washing-up liquid v**e**ro
wasp os**a**
watch *(wristwatch)* r**u**chen chas**o**vnik
    (verb) nablyood**a**vam
water vod**a**
waterfall vodop**a**t
water heater nagrev**a**tel za vod**a**
wave *(noun)* vuln**a**
    (verb: with hand) m**a**Ham
wavy *(hair)* na vuln**i**
we n**i**-eh
weather vr**e**meh
wedding sv**a**dba
week s**e**dmitsa
welcome *(verb)* doshl**i**
  you're welcome m**o**lya
wellingtons g**oo**meni bot**oo**shi
Welsh w**e**lski

Welshman welsets
were: we were ni-eh byaHmeh
  you were vi-eh byaHteh
  (singular, familiar) ti besheh
  they were teh byaHa
west zapat
wet mokur
what? kakvo?
wheel kolelo
wheelchair invalidna kolichka
when? koga?
where? kudeh?
whether dali
which? koy?
whisky wiski
white byal
who? koy?
why? zashto?
wide shirok
wife suprooga, zhena
wind vyatur
window prozorets
windscreen predno stuklo
wine vino
wine list menyoo za vinata
wine merchant turgovets na
  vino
wing krilo
with s
without bes
woman zhena
wood *(material)* durvo
wool vulna
word dooma
work *(noun)* rabota
  (verb) rabotya
worse po losho
worst nI losho

wrapping paper Harti-ya za
  oovivaneh, ambalazhna Harti-ya
wrist kitka
writing paper listi za pisma
wrong greshen

year godina
yellow zhult
yes da
yesterday fchera
yet: is it ready yet? gotovo li eh
  vecheh?
  not yet neh oshteh
yoghurt kiselo mlyako
you vi-eh
  (singular, familiar) ti
your: your friend vashi-ya pri-
  yatel
  (familiar) tvo-ya pri-yatel
  your book vashata kniga
  (familiar) tvo-yata kniga
  your seat vasheto myasto
  (familiar) tvo-eto myasto
  your shoes vashiteh oboofki
  (familiar) tvo-iteh oboofki
yours: is this yours? tova vasheh
  li eh?
  (familiar) tova tvo-eh li eh?
youth hostel stoodentsko
  opshtezhiti-eh
Yugoslavia yoogoslavi-ya
Yugoslavian yoogoslafski

zip tsip
zoo zo-ologicheska gradina, zo-
  opark